*Advance praise*

# Nāgārjuna's Wisdom

"With these luminous and carefully constructed explanations, Barry Kerzin offers us the vast and profound insights of his teachers on one of the most fundamental Buddhist texts elucidating the nature of reality, Nāgārjuna's famed *Fundamental Verses on the Middle Way*. With loving patience and enthusiasm, he helps us recognize the way suffering arises and guides us through the process to uproot its deep-seated causes through lucid reasoning and wisdom: a must-read for anyone who wishes to gain a genuine understanding of Buddhist philosophy and practice."
—Matthieu Ricard, translator of *Enlightened Vagabond* and *The Life of Shabkar: The Autobiography of a Tibetan Yogin*

"Venerable Barry's wonderful book on the Middle Way is especially valuable as his unique personal transmission of His Holiness the Dalai Lama's way of opening the door into Nāgārjuna's masterwork. Its twenty-seven critiques, deconstructing everything in the universe, from causation via self and nirvāṇa all the way to worldviews, are the arch pattern of the meditation on emptiness and compassion. Ven. Barry channels His Holiness and leads us right into it. His work is to be cherished."
—Professor Robert Thurman, Columbia University

"With guidance from classical commentaries and oral instructions of great Tibetan teachers, and relating these to decades of meditative reflection, Venerable Barry Kerzin offers a remarkable guide to the key insights and reasoning that are at the heart of Nāgārjuna's famed Middle Way philosophy. Thanks to this book, any serious Buddhist practitioner can now appreciate why the Tibetan tradition makes so much fuss about Nāgārjuna and his wisdom."

—Thupten Jinpa, principal English translator to His Holiness the Dalai Lama and author of *Self, Reality, and Reason in Tibetan Philosophy*

"Dr. Barry Kerzin articulates a crisp and clearheaded analysis of key concepts—like 'emptiness,' conventional and ultimate reality, and 'self'—for those of us who so easily muddy them. In *Nāgārjuna's Wisdom* he kindly offers us clarity to sweep away our confusion."

—Daniel Goleman, author of *A Force for Good: The Dalai Lama's Vision for the World*

"Nāgārjuna's *Fundamental Verses on the Middle Way*, the basis of Madhyamaka thought, is a profound but difficult philosophical text. One can work so hard to understand the ideas that the relevance to practice may not be apparent. Nonetheless, this text is indispensable to Mahāyāna Buddhist practice. In this volume, Barry Kerzin offers a

discussion that is precise but highly readable, one that reflects Dr. Kerzin's years of study with great Tibetan masters."
—Jay Garfield, Doris Silbert Professor in the Humanities, Smith College and the Harvard Divinity School

"My longtime spiritual brother, the US doctor Barry Kerzin, has written a succinct book on Madhyamaka philosophy and its background, historical development, and critique of the different schools within a limited space of less than three hundred pages for general and seasoned readers. I am confident of its immense benefit to whoever goes through it, as it contains the wisdom of a great Tibetan Buddhist master, Gen Wangchen-la, whose depth and breadth of Buddhist knowledge and modern science was without limit. This book confidently traverses the terrain of philosophy from an Indo-Tibetan perspective that is closer to the concept of nonobjectivity in things well-known in quantum physics. I hope the readers would comprehend the wisdom of parallelism between emptiness and dependent arising from this work."
—Tenzin Tsepag, English translator for His Holiness Dalai Lama

"Barry Kerzin, a physician turned Tibetan Buddhist monk, brings alive key portions of the extraordinary treatise of the great Buddhist philosopher Nāgārjuna, the *Fundamental Verses of the Middle Way*, in this accessible book. This is a practical guide to understanding one of the most important insights in the Buddhist tradition— emptiness—and helps the average reader appreciate the relevance of this realization to everyday life. A must-read for anyone interested in Buddhist philosophy or psychology."

—Richard J. Davidson, director, Center for Healthy Minds, University of Wisconsin–Madison, coauthor of *Altered Traits*

"I cannot speak authoritatively about a subject so deep and the pyrotechnics of its logic so incisive that I stand in awe at what the author has done under the guidance of His Holiness the Dalai Lama and his other teachers. But my impression is that *Nāgārjuna's Wisdom* is analytical meditation at its best—a pointer for all who care deeply to recognize our habitual dualistic tendencies as intrinsically incomplete, inaccurate, and ignoring of what is most fundamental. Here is *prajñā pāramitā*, wisdom beyond wisdom, mapped out in its full expression, to whatever degree it is even possible to use words to point beyond words. Like the sun, be prepared to burn if you get too close. In this case, what will be illuminated and then incinerated are your attachments—to anything, including who you think you are. And this cannot but be of benefit to all."

—Jon Kabat-Zinn, author of *Falling Awake* and *The Healing Power of Mindfulness*

"I learned so much from this methodical, vernacular lesson in the Middle Way from one of the Dalai Lama's most trusted emissaries."

—Fred de Sam Lazaro, correspondent, *PBS NewsHour*, and executive director, Undertold Stories Project

# Nāgārjuna's Wisdom

*A Practitioner's Guide
to the Middle Way*

BARRY KERZIN, MD

Wisdom Publications
199 Elm Street
Somerville, MA 02144 USA
wisdompubs.org

*Library of Congress Cataloging-in-Publication Data*
Names: Kerzin, Barry, author.
Title: Nāgārjuna's wisdom: a practitioner's guide to the Middle Way / Barry
Kerzin, MD.
Description: Somerville, MA: Wisdom Publications, [2019] | Includes
bibliographical references and index. |
Identifiers: LCCN 2018020830 (print) | LCCN 2018053733 (ebook) |
ISBN 9781614295198 (e-book) | ISBN 9781614294993 (pbk.: alk. paper) |
ISBN 9781614295198 (ebook)
Subjects: LCSH: Nāgārjuna, active 2nd century. Madhyamakakārikā—
Commentaries. | Mādhyamika (Buddhism) | Buddhist philosophy.
Classification: LCC BQ2797 (ebook) | LCC BQ2797 .K47 2019 (print) |
DDC 294.3/85—dc23
LC record available at https://lccn.loc.gov/2018020830

ISBN 978-1-61429-499-3     ebook ISBN 978-1-61429-519-8

23 22 21 20 19     5  4  3  2  1

Cover design by Graciela Galup.
Interior design by Greta D. Sibley. Set in Garamond Premier Pro.

Printed in the United States of America.

# PUBLISHER'S ACKNOWLEDGMENT

The publisher gratefully acknowledges the generous help of the Hershey Family Foundation in sponsoring the production of this book.

# CONTENTS

# Contents

# FOREWORD

*by His Holiness the Dalai Lama*

Nāgārjuna was the preeminent scholar of the Nālandā tradition. His writings reveal his great qualities; he was precise and profound. His followers, Āryadeva, Bhāvaviveka, Buddhapālita, and Candrakīrti elaborated on what he wrote. Nāgārjuna praised the Buddha not only for attaining enlightenment but also specifically for teaching dependent arising. In a final tribute at the end of *Fundamental Verses on the Middle Way* he wrote that the Buddha taught as he did to rid sentient beings of all distorted views.

The *Fundamental Verses on the Middle Way* is Nāgārjuna's key work, in which he demonstrates that phenomena are empty of inherent existence because they are dependent on other factors. He clearly indicates that the view that phenomena do not inherently exist is not nihilistic, as some critics assert, but that their functionality is in fact due to their being empty of any aspect of inherent existence.

*Fundamental Verses on the Middle Way* is a book I have read and studied closely for more than sixty years; it's like an old friend. When I introduce it to others there are certain chapters I recommend they begin with. Readers who make themselves familiar with chapters 26, 18, 24, and 22 will come to understand how we fall into cyclic existence, how there is no independently existent self, and how things have no objective existence but are dependently arisen.

This book, *Nāgārjuna's Wisdom*, had its origins in an explanation of *Fundamental Verses on the Middle Way* given to Dr. Barry Kerzin by Geshé Namgyal Wangchen, a learned and experienced teacher from the Drepung Loseling Monastery.

Dr. Kerzin, an American monk, has been a student of Buddhism for thirty years. Following the pattern of the Nālandā tradition, he has studied this text, reflected on what it means, and meditated on what he has understood. Here he has presented some of what he has understood. I have no doubt that readers who would like to know more about Nāgārjuna's point of view will benefit from a reading of this book.

14 May 2019

# PREFACE

When I was fourteen years old my world was shaken. I read D. T. Suzuki, something about how words create our reality, and my head turned 360 degrees. I was stunned. How could this be?

I spent the next few years trying to find out. First there was philosophy club in high school, and then there was study as a philosophy major at the University of California at Berkeley. More questions arose. I was far from satiated. I applied for and was admitted into a PhD philosophy/ humanistic psychology program to continue this pursuit, but at the last minute plans changed and I went to medical school instead. Yet the hunger persisted. How could everything I took to be so tangible and true be the result of words, language, and concepts, as I read in the Zen text?

So, years later, a doctor, I moved to India full of questions, hungry for answers. After many years of meditation retreats the questions had calmed down, but hadn't fully resolved. Answers seemed one day clear, but the next day confused. On my third trip to India, beginning my three-decade stay there, at a converted embassy-cum-rose-garden guesthouse in Delhi, I met a special friend who would later teach me what may be the most famous and profound text explaining Buddhist wisdom in detail: Nāgārjuna's *Fundamental Verses on the Middle Way*.

Gen Namgyal Wangchen was a master. He studied for his geshé exam,[1] but rather than take the test, he decided to go up to the mountains and meditate instead. This was a real practitioner. After having spent more than a decade teaching in the United Kingdom, he had returned to his home away from home in south India at Drepung Loseling Monastery in his Phara Khangtshen house.

To my great joy Gen Wangchen accepted my request to teach me the *Fundamental Verses on the Middle Way*. For two-month periods over five consecutive winters he taught me this classic text verse by verse, sometimes in English, sometimes in Tibetan. When Gen Wanghen taught in Tibetan, the extremely kind and learned Tenzin Tsepag was my translator. I am deeply grateful for his help not only in translating but also in reviewing the material after the sessions. My Tibetan is not good enough to understand all the technical nuances.

After the teachings were completed, I spent the next several years transcribing Gen Wangchen's commentary

and some of my own reflections, and then editing everything to create this book. Translations of Nāgārjuna's text
were done by myself and Tenzin Tsepag.[2] At first, there
were between 800–900 pages. Several publishing houses
rejected my manuscript, saying it was much too long. So I
tried editing it down, but I couldn't get very far. Dejected,
I put the manuscript aside. Several years later Professor
Robert Thurman took an interest. If we could pare it
down, Columbia University Press might be interested in
publishing it. But how could we reduce nearly 900 pages to
250? Then a stroke of genius came from Bob. He suggested
that we not publish commentaries for all the twenty-
seven chapters of *Fundamental Verses on the Middle Way*.
Rather, we would be selective. But how could we de-
cide which of the many pith and wonderful chapters in
Nāgārjuna's seminal work to leave aside?

Then it dawned on us. For years His Holiness the
Dalai Lama had been encouraging me to publish this commentary. We should make a commentary following the
approach he uses when he teaches this classic text! His
Holiness often selects the same five chapters—chapters 26,
18, 24, 22, and 1, in that order—because these five chapters
contain the pith and marrow of Buddhist philosophy.

This light-bulb-on moment made the manuscript
workable, bringing it down to a manageable page length
through commenting only on these five chapters. I am
deeply appreciative and grateful to Professor Thurman

not only for his brilliant idea of how to reduce the manuscript size but also for believing in me.

Then the real work began. I am not much of a scholar, and I didn't want to make this a pseudoscholarly work. Instead, I have tried wherever possible to make this commentary helpful to practitioners. This, I feel, is my debt owed to the late master Gen Wangchen. And this is the reason I believe students of Nāgārjuna and the Buddhadharma who genuinely yearn for an end to life's incessant conceptual and emotional pain will read this book.

As the editing progressed, Professor Jay Garfield took a great interest in helping me every step of the way. My gratitude is immense for this remarkable scholar and friend, for his patience and kindness in answering every question with clarity and insight.

I am grateful to Geshe Ngawang Sonam for helping to clarify difficult points in the translation of the root text from Tibetan into English and some difficult points in the commentary.

Most of all, this work would never have been possible without the deep kindness and care from the master of masters, His Holiness the Dalai Lama. He has nurtured me for nearly thirty years now. My love for my late mother and late wife, both of whom died early, has naturally transferred the Dalai Lama. This love has grown exponentially. The only way I know to thank him is to try my very best to follow his example. Thus I write this book dedicating it to unlimited happiness for all living beings—for this is what his life and lives are all about.

Many others have helped produce this book along the way. Gratitude to Yangten Rinpoché for clarifying difficult points, and to my friend, the great teacher Gen Gyatso at the Institute of Buddhist Dialectics in Dharamsala, for providing much background material. For my friend Ratö Khen Rinpoché, Nicky Vreeland, I have much appreciation and warmth for his encouragement and early suggestions during the long evolution of this manuscript, as well as for his monastic guidance. Finally, in the later and most important part of this process, I have deep gratitude to Wisdom Publications for agreeing to publish this work. Daniel Aitken, the publisher and CEO at Wisdom Publications, has graciously accepted my request. Deep thanks to him. Laura Cunningham, the editor, has been a gem. We work together with warmth and humor, although she gave me much work to do! Nevertheless, I am indebted to her clarity and vision. There have been many others whose names are too numerous to mention.

I am lucky. Even though my mother died quite early, she was indeed a warm, kind, and loving mother. This has allowed me to open my heart to others. His Holiness the Dalai Lama has raised the ante—encouraging me to open my heart not just to others, but to *all* others. This book is dedicated to him and them.

# Introduction

Nāgārjuna's *Fundamental Verses on the Middle Way*, or as it's known in Tibetan, *Root Wisdom*, is the definitive presentation of the doctrine of emptiness and dependent arising and a foundational text of Mahāyāna Buddhism.[3] It is referred to as *Wisdom* because it is based on the perfection of wisdom (*prajñāpāramitā*) sūtras of the Buddha, which discuss the wisdom of emptiness in detail. This book will follow the way the present Dalai Lama teaches it—a method that introduces us to Buddhist philosophy step by step, in an order conducive to practice.

His Holiness starts with chapter 26, "Analysis of the Twelve Links of Dependent Origination," which explains how we enter cyclic existence (saṃsāra) and how we exit (to nirvāṇa). We perpetuate saṃsāra through following the links in the forward order, and we put an end to saṃsāra through following the links in the reverse order. We enter and sustain saṃsāra through ignorance; we exit saṃsāra through eliminating ignorance by realizing emptiness.

One might get the misleading impression from chapter 26 that there is a real self that cycles in and (potentially) leaves saṃsāra. In order to correct this potential error, the Dalai Lama then explains chapter 18, "Analysis of the Self," which refutes the idea that there is an intrinsically existent self.

From this, some might then get the false idea that there is no person at all. This is because most people cannot differentiate between the absence of intrinsic existence and complete nonexistence. To avert this potential misunderstanding, the Dalai Lama teaches chapter 24, "Analysis of the Four Noble Truths," which establishes conventional reality, including a conventional person.

In chapter 24, Nāgārjuna argues that he does not undermine, but explains, the four noble truths and the Three Jewels; he argues they make sense only in the context of emptiness. Thus, he argues, conventional reality makes sense not because things exist intrinsically, but because they do not—they exist only as empty.

Some might then make the mistake of thinking that emptiness itself exists intrinsically. To counter this potential tendency to reify emptiness, the Dalai Lama teaches chapter 22, "Analysis of the Tathāgata." Here Nāgārjuna establishes that everything—including emptiness—is empty. So emptiness itself has no special ontological status, and this empty nature of the world allows everything to unfold.

When time permits, the Dalai Lama then teaches chapter 1, "Analysis of Conditions." This chapter refutes the intrinsic production of anything anywhere at any time. The scope of emptiness is unlimited; nowhere is there anything at any time that is not empty.

This method of teaching the text reflects an idea that Tsongkhapa advances in the first chapter of his *Ocean of Reasoning: A Great Commentary on Nāgārjuna's Fundamental Verses on the Middle Way* (*Dbu ma rtsa ba tshig le'ur byas pa shes rab ces bya ba'i rnam bshad rigs pa'i rgya mtsho*). There he presents several sequences in which to read the text—including one very similar to the order adopted by the Dalai Lama. Tsongkhapa calls this the chapter sequence based on the two selflessnesses: that of the person and that of phenomena. We can see the Dalai Lama's preferred sequence as reflecting this interpretative framework.

The key difference between this order and His Holiness's is that Tsongkhapa skips over chapter 26, "Analysis of the Twelve Links of Dependent Origination," and begins by explaining chapter 18, "Analysis of the Self." After the intrinsic self (person) is thoroughly analyzed and refuted, he then turns to analyzing phenomena. Tsongkhapa next summarizes chapter 24, which he reads as a defense of conventional reality in response to the charge that Nāgārjuna is a nihilist. Tsongkhapa then argues that chapter 22 is Nāgārjuna's argument that even the enlightened one (that is, the Buddha) has no special existential status and that emptiness itself is also empty of intrinsic existence. All compounded phenomena exist in the causal nexus. For this reason, the next chapter in Tsongkhapa's sequence of Nāgārjuna's *Fundamental Verses on the Middle Way* is chapter 1, the refutation of intrinsic production. Causality is the central relationship between things in an evolving world. The causal relation underlies change, and so grounds impermanence.

In this volume, I've included an appendix: twenty verses on *bodhicitta* from Nāgārjuna's *Precious Advice for a King* (*Ratnāvalī*) that remind us why we are crunching our brains and minds to understand emptiness; it is to benefit all others in the deepest and fullest ways. These twenty verses are inspiring and arouse our universal compassion.

## Nāgārjuna

According to the Indian and Tibetan Buddhist tradition, the Buddha prophesized in the *Descent into Laṅkā Sūtra* (*Laṅkāvatāra Sūtra*) that Nāgārjuna would uphold his teachings. In this text, Buddha is said to have stated that Nāgārjuna would be born in South India, called the Land of the Vedas. He would be called by the bhikṣu name Śrī, and his common name would be Nāga.

Furthermore, according to the *Descent into Laṅkā Sūtra*, the Buddha stated that Nāgārjuna would explain his teachings by destroying the notions of *existence* and *nonexistence*. In that way he would clearly delineate the distinction between *existence* and *intrinsic existence* on the one hand, and between *nonexistence* and *nonintrinsic existence* on the other hand. Similar statements are attributed to the Buddha in the *Sublime Golden Light Sūtra* (*Suvarṇaprabhāsottama Sūtra*).

In the *Root Tantra of Mañjuśrī* (*Mañjuśrīmūlatantra*), the Buddha is said to have stated that Nāgārjuna would live six hundred years. In the *Great Drum Sūtra* (*Mahābherīhāraka Sūtra*), however, the Buddha is said to have stated that a youthful bhikṣu named Nāgārjuna would be born eighty years after the Buddha's passing and would contribute to the flourishing of the Buddha's teachings by living one hundred years. Afterward, he was to pass into the Pure Land of Sukhāvatī, the Land of Bliss. In both the *Great Cloud Sūtra* (*Mahāmegha Sūtra*) and the *Great Drum Sūtra* the Buddha is said to have stated that Nāgārjuna would later be enlightened. In the tantric discourse called *Illuminating Lamp* (*Pradīpoddyotana*) the Buddha is said to have stated that Nāgārjuna would achieve the enlightenment of a *vajradhāra*[4] in that very lifetime. Furthermore, he is said to have stated that Nāgārjuna would become enlightened through the practice of the highest yoga tantra (Skt. *anuttarayoga tantra*, Tib. *bla na med pa'i rgyud*). The Dalai Lama cautions us not to view these citations as contradictory, for they may not be presented from a historical perspective.

Indeed, little is known about Nāgārjuna's actual life. Although there is no lack of literary sources discussing Nāgārjuna, almost all the elements contained therein are mythical at best and conflicting at worst. Most of the material comes from accounts that were written with hagio-graphical interests ahead of historical documentation. Clearly, for those who like certainty, any kind of "proof" of Nāgārjuna's dates and place of residency is still a long way off. Nonetheless, citing a wealth of archeological, art historical, and textual evidence, Joseph Walser (2005) makes a remarkably persuasive case for Nāgārjuna to have lived in the late second century in the lower Krishna valley, in the present state of Karnataka.

Nāgārjuna composed many texts. Chief among them are the six texts on emptiness: his opus *Fundamental Verses on the Middle Way*, *Reply to Objections* (*Vigrahavyāvartanī*), *Seventy Verses on Emptiness* (*Śūnyatāsaptati*), *Sixty Verses of Reasoning* (*Yuktiṣaṣṭikā*), *Devastating Discourse* (*Vaidalyaprakaraṇa*), and *Precious Garland of Advice to a King* (*Ratnāvalī*).

In *Reply to Objections*, Nāgārjuna establishes that, even though everything is devoid of intrinsic existence, it is still possible to use logic to refute others' mistaken views.

In *Seventy Verses on Emptiness*, Nāgārjuna further explores the two truths. He explains how phenomena exist based on worldly conventions, despite the fact that they do not exist intrinsically. In his *Sixty Verses*, Nāgārjuna applies this to the path to awakening, arguing that it is necessary for the attainment of liberation to realize the distinction between existence and intrinsic existence on the one hand, and between nonexistence and nonintrinsic existence on the other hand.

The *Devastating Discourse* is a polemical text that argues for the incoherence of the conceptual categories of the Nyāya school.

In his *Precious Garland of Advice to a King*, Nāgārjuna explains to the king that devotion and faith to a wholesome way of life is required for rebirth in the human or higher realms. Devotion inspires one to listen, understand, and apply the teachings on wisdom to one's own emotional and cognitive life, leading to liberation and enlightenment. This text also explores the moral and political dimensions of his Madhyamaka thought.

Attributions of *One Hundred Preparations* (*Sbyor ba brgya pa*), various other texts on medical science, and other texts about tantra to Nāgārjuna are doubtful.

Nāgārjuna is also said to have composed a set of hymns of praise (*stotras*), which pay homage to and explain emptiness and dependent origination, and explain how to avoid falling into the two extreme views of intrinsic existence and nonexistence. Although there is controversy regarding their authorship, the Dalai Lama seems to accept the hymns as authentic.[5]

## The Logic of the *Fundamental Verses on the Middle Way*

We see certain patterns of logical analysis repeated again and again in *Fundamental Verses on the Middle Way*. Each time, the opponent takes something to be intrinsically real, and then Nāgārjuna employs one of several methods of refutation to prove that it is not.

One method Nāgārjuna often employs is a *destructive dilemma*, showing that pairs of things the opponent takes to exist intrinsically can be neither identical to nor different from one another. Nāgārjuna also uses a second, similar strategy—the negative *tetralemma*—for this purpose.[6]

A third argument template is a *trilemma*: the three temporal periods. The future is yet to come. The past has already been. And the present cannot be found. As finely as you can divide, the present cannot be found. It is still either past or future and *only* exists in dependence on the past and the future. This logic is used extensively in chapter 2, "Analysis of Motion," examining when and where the walker walks.

A fourth argument form is the *infinite*. For example, if all existent things have the three characteristics of originating, enduring, and disintegrating, then what about origination itself? Does it too have all three characteristics? Since it is an existent thing, it must. But then we fall into a vicious infinite regress. This is the argument pursued in chapter 7, "Analysis of Arising, Abiding, and Disintegration."

Fifth, Nāgārjuna uses the argument *refuting reflexivity*. This is used to refute a claim that something bears a relationship to itself. For example, a knife cannot cut itself. Nor can darkness cover itself. Nor can a finger point at itself. This argument likewise is pursued in chapter 7.

Sixth is the argument from *mutual dependence*. This refutes the assumption that things exist intrinsically by showing that they exist in mutual dependence. This argument is presented mainly in chapter 10, "Analysis of Fire and Fuel," verse 10.

All these logical arguments Nāgārjuna presents are for understanding the distinctions between existence and intrinsic existence, and nonexistence and nonintrinsic existence. Understanding these distinctions is crucial for understanding the lack of intrinsic existence, and hence emptiness.

## The Question of Existence

In addition to gaining familiarity with the logical techniques Nāgārjuna employs in *Fundamental Verses on the Middle Way*, it is also crucial to clearly understand two distinctions: the one between *existence* and *intrinsic existence* and the one between *nonexistence* and *nonintrinsic existence*. To refute intrinsic existence does not mean to refute the existence of things. To confuse these is to confuse the doctrine of emptiness with nihilism.

In the prajñāpāramitā sūtras the Buddha draws these distinctions explicitly. When he argues that each of a list of 108 phenomena "do not exist," he immediately qualifies this by saying they "*do not exist ultimately.*"

In chapter 15, verse 7, Nāgārjuna writes:

**7. The Blessed One through
understanding entity and nonentity,
in the *Discourse to Kātyāyana*,
refuted both existence and nonexistence.**

In the *Discourse to Kātyāyana* (*Kātyāyanāvavāda*), the Buddha tells Kātyāyana that his path is the middle path between the two extreme views of existence and nonexistence. He also eschews the two extremes in the *Anavatapta Sūtra*:

> The wise, having understood dependently originated
> phenomena, do not rely on extreme views.
> They understand that phenomena have causes and
> conditions,
> and that no phenomena exist without causes and
> conditions.[7]

Nāgārjuna repeatedly demonstrates the Buddha's teachings on reality to be free of ultimate nature in a similar fashion to the way the Buddha does in his extensive prajñāpāramitā teachings, for instance in the *108 Topics* (*Aṣṭādaśapaṭalavistaravyākhyā*) where he qualifies "not exist" to mean "not to exist ultimately."

In chapter 24, verse 14, Nāgārjuna writes:

> 14. To whom emptiness makes sense
> everything makes sense.
> To whom emptiness does not make sense
> nothing makes sense.

This implies that an understanding of emptiness as emptiness of intrinsic existence, as opposed to emptiness of existence, is necessary in order to understand the nature of reality.

Thus, the reality of things is not denied within emptiness. It is just the opposite, in fact; within emptiness, things are present in the causal nexus. They are dynamic and they function. They relate to each other and they change. This potential for transformation allows us to become better human beings, guide others to do the same, and eventually become enlightened.

## Identifying the Object of Negation

There are two types of object of negation. There is the object of negation of the mind (the subjective objective of negation) and the object of negation through reasoning (the objective object of negation). This is according to Tsongkhapa. Self-grasping is the object of negation of mind: it exists. It is the basis for us wandering in samsara. The intrinsic self is the object of negation through reasoning: it does not exist. In order to eliminate the object of negation of mind (self-grasping), we have to logically use reasoning to establish the absence of the objective object of negation. Candrakīrti in *Entering the Middle Way* (*Madhyamakāvatāra*) says this:

> That all faults such as afflictions come from the view
> (Grasping at) perishable collection, seeing this with
> mind
> And realizing that self is the object of this,
> The yogi will engage in the negation of this
> (intrinsic) self.

Buddhapālita, an important early commentator who lived after Nāgārjuna, tells us that if something were intrinsically existent, then we should always be able to point to it directly, and clearly identify it. But this is impossible. Pinpointing the exact thing is elusive. For there is no thingness, no *whole without parts*, that persists independently from all other things. Thus we cannot point directly to such a thing for such an intrinsic thing does not exist. Take, for example, a car. Point precisely to the car. Your finger points to the side of the car that's facing you, perhaps the left side. But what about the right side? If your finger points to the top of the car, what about the bottom? If the pointing finger circles around the whole outside of the car, what about the inside? The more we try to precisely point to the actual car, the more elusive it gets. This is precisely what Buddhapālita means when he says if something were intrinsically existent, then at all times we must be able to point to it directly, and clearly identify it. But we can't. Therefore, any and all intrinsically existing entities do not exist.

In *Ocean of Reasoning*, Tsongkhapa introduces the term *object of negation* (*dgag bya*); to understand the subtle nature of reality we must first know what it is not. We want to eliminate, or negate, false superimposition, in order to correctly understand reality. In the case of Madhyamaka analysis, the object of negation is neither *mere existence*, nor *the appearing object itself*, but rather *intrinsic existence*.

We must differentiate the basis for the object of negation and the object of negation itself. For instance, if we look at the chariot in Candrakīrti's famous analogy from *Entering the Middle Way*—in which we are asked to determine where, among all the parts of a chariot, or even separate from the parts, its essential chariot nature is—the chariot is the basis on which we impute the object of negation. But even though we impute the object of negation upon its basis, we do not negate the basis of the object of negation, only the object of negation. We do not negate the chariot, but only its intrinsic existence. Thus there is only one object of negation—intrinsic existence. When we thoroughly eliminate the object of negation, the aggregates that form the basis for the imputation of self will not be apprehended as existing intrinsically. We will continue seeing the conventionally existent person, but the intrinsic nature that we falsely impute will be negated.[8]

It is necessary to distinguish two things—the appearing object (*snang yul*) and the conceptually grasped object (*zhen yul*). First there is the appearance of the object. Then there is clinging to the conceptually grasped object of our conception. The referent object is not the basis of designation. The conceptually grasped object or the intrinsic self is not consistent with reality. Rather it is what we falsely conceive in the mind.

The basis of designation for the designated object, cup, is all of its parts including the handle, lip, and container. The designated object is the cup. These two are mutually dependent. Because they are mutually dependent, neither of these can exist independently. Although at the sensorial level there is the appearance of intrinsic existence, the sensorial consciousness does not have the ability to *ascertain* intrinsic existence. This is because sensorial consciousness does not have the capacity to discern, label, or assert. This intellectual capacity is reserved only for the mental consciousness. Therefore, the appearance of intrinsic existence to the sensory consciousness comes about due to our habitual grasping at intrinsic existence that occurs at the mental consciousness level. This grasping mental consciousness infects all of our minds including the sensorial minds.

When objects appear to our ordinary mind, they appear as intrinsically existent. This mistaken aspect of the mind, where there is the appearance of intrinsically existent object, is cognitive obscuration. Its complete elimination occurs only when we become completely enlightened. However, when objects appear as intrinsically existent to us, one part of our mind grasps at this intrinsic object. This grasping becomes the basis of all negative emotions. The complete elimination of this grasping at intrinsic object occurs even before enlightenment, sometime after nonconceptually realizing (direct) emptiness.

It is crucial to understand the distinction between a mistaken (*'khrul shes*) and a wrong (*log shes*) mind. A mistaken mind's object of appearance does not exist. A wrong mind's object of engagement also does not exist. In order to understand the mistaken aspect of the mind, it is important to recognize what the appearing object of the mind actually is. Generally, there are two kinds of minds, sensorial and mental. Objects appearing directly to sensorial minds are their appearing objects (*snang yul*). Take, for example, a cup that appears to a visual consciousness. This is the *snang yul*, or appearing object of that visual consciousness. The object of engagement, *'jug yul*, is the apprehended object. With respect to a visual consciousness perceiving a cup, the cup is both its object of appearance and object of engagement. However, when something appears to the visual consciousness but fails to be apprehended, there is only the object of appearance and not the object of engagement. An example is when you are mentally absorbed and something appears to your visual consciousness but is not apprehended. The same understanding is true for all the other four sensorial consciousnesses. Our gross mental consciousness, which is a conceptual mind, has as an appearing object and a conceptually grasped object (*zheng yul*). In classical epistemological Buddhist texts, appearing objects are attributable to all types of minds, whereas conceptually grasped objects are reserved for only conceptual minds. Objects of engagement, or apprehended objects, apply to all minds. The referent (focal) object, that is, *dmigs yul*, is the object to which the mind is directed. When a mind focuses on the referent object, what appears to it becomes its appearing object (*snang yul*), while what it apprehends becomes its object of engagement (*'jug yul*). Both the appearing object (*snang yul*) and the object of engagement (*'jug yul*) are universal for all minds. Regarding self-grasping of a person, the person is the referent (focal) object (*dmig yul*), whereas the intrinsic self is both the appearing object (*snang yul*) as well as the conceptually grasped object (*zhen yul*). Self-grasping is a mistaken and wrong perception that binds us to samsara and is the root of all our delusions. That is why self-grasping is the objection of negation and must be eliminated completely from its root.

When searching for the object of negation, we may get some understanding that nothing is there and go too far with our analysis into nihilistic waters. We may become frightened feeling that something familiar is totally missing, that "I" do not exist at all. If this happens, it is important to retreat from nihilism a little, avoiding the precipice of annihilation.

## Synonyms for Intrinsic Existence

From the Prāsaṅgika Madhyamaka perspective there are a number of synonyms for independent existence (*rang dbang gis grub pa*), intrinsic (or inherent) existence (*rang bzhin gyis grub pa*), existent from the side of the object (*rang ngos nas grub pa*), true existence (*bden par grub pa*), existing by its own nature (*rang gi ngo bos grub pa*), and existing by its own characteristics (*rang gi mtshan nyid kyis grub pa*). These are different terms with the same meaning. They all suggest some kind of intrinsicality, essence, or real entity, and all of them are mentioned in Candrakīrti's *Clear Words* (*Prasannapadā*), another commentary on Nāgārjuna's *Fundamental Verses*. These different terms refer to the object to be negated when establishing emptiness.

Tsongkhapa utilizes the same terms and phrases for the object of negation, but he also uses a new term: *btags don btsal na brnyed pa ltar* or "as if you could find the designated object, or referent, when searched for," which is not found in the works of Nāgārjuna, Candrakīrti, or the other great Indian masters. Tsongkhapa discusses this notion in several of his texts, notably in *Essence of Eloquent Interpretation* (*Drang nges legs bshad snying po*) and the special insight section of *The Great Treatise on the Stages of the Path to Enlightenment* (*Lam rim lhag mthong chen mo*). When we look for an intrinsic entity, we have the sense we can find it. If anything did exist intrinsically, then it should be possible, upon analysis, to find that thing. But we can't ever do this; so nothing exists in that way. The object of negation is the intrinsic identity that should be, but is not, revealed by analysis.

This *mistaken* sense that intrinsic nature must be present is the novel perspective presented by Tsongkhapa.

Likewise, Paṇchen Sönam Drakpa[10] and other great scholars have coined another new term: not being satisfied with mere imputation (*btags tsam gyis ma tshim pa*). In other words, the term means suspecting there is something more than what is merely imputed.

Denma Tongpoen Rinpoché[11] wrote a text called *Domain of Reality According to Madhyamaka* (*Dbu ma chos dbyings*). There he mentioned that it is very difficult to express in words the object of negation, which when negated evokes the clear understanding of emptiness. Therefore, in order to clarify and precisely identify the object of negation, past masters have used a variety of terms to express the same meaning for the object of negation in order to understand emptiness precisely. Different terms add slightly different nuances from slightly different perspectives, bringing more breadth and precision to the understanding.

This is similar to looking at the same thing from different angles or perspectives; by doing so one gets a more complete picture. Due to people's varying mental dispositions, some will understand the object of negation (the mistaken view of reality) using the term *rang bzhin gyis grub pa*, meaning *intrinsic existence*. Others will understand the term *rang gi ngo bos grub pa*, meaning *from its own side*, more clearly, and so forth. Even a single individual at different times will resonate with a different term. Thus, knowledge of all the different terms used for the object of negation gives us wider breadth when reflecting and meditating on emptiness.

The Amdo master Jigmé Damchö's[12] commentary on Tsongkhapa's *Essence of Eloquent Interpretation* lists all these different terms used for the object of negation. He concludes that whichever term suits the practitioner's disposition and brings the object of negation into sharp focus should be used by the practitioner for the purpose of gaining insight. This suggests some flexibility regarding the choice of the accepted term for the object of negation depending on one's understanding.

Sometimes the object of negation is clear using little effort. At other times the object of negation is not clear, despite using much effort. At those difficult times, it seems best to use a different accepted term for the object of negation, or to use different reasoning for refuting intrinsic existence. The understanding of the view of emptiness may not stay the same. At one time we may find ourselves becoming very clear about the understanding of the view, whereas after several days, if we try to recapture that same experience, it may not return.

This is not only true with the view of emptiness but is also true regarding all the points of the path, for example, impermanence and death. At one time we may have a very special experience of one of the points of the path. It may be clear, and we feel *this* is it. The experience may be intense with conviction. A few days later we may think we can go back to that experience, but it is unlikely. Therefore, we need constant familiarization with understanding and experience. Familiarizing our minds repeatedly by meditating on the different points of the path, our experience and understanding become more stable.

## The Eight Extreme Understandings of Dependent Origination

In the salutation at the beginning of the *Fundamental Verses on the Middle Way*, Nāgārjuna rejects eight extreme understandings of dependent origination.

> **I prostrate to the perfect Buddha,**
> **the best of all teachers,**
> **who taught that dependent origination is**
> **free of cessation, and free of production,**
> **without disintegration, and without permanence,**
> **without coming, and without going,**
> **without distinction or oneness,**
> **and peaceful in total extinction**
> **of all conceptual fabrications.**

Nāgārjuna chooses these particular eight extremes to open his text because they are precisely the views used by those who think to exist is to be nonempty, and to be empty is to not exist, in their attempts to establish intrinsic existence. These views also reflect how dependent origination is characterized in the Sarvāstivādin Abhidharma. To say that things are dependently arisen is to say that they arise and cease, that they come to be and disintegrate, that they come into existence and go out of existence, and that they are the same as their constituents ultimately but different conventionally. Nāgārjuna rejects these views through ultimate analysis, although he accepts them conventionally.

Those who think that to exist is to be nonempty and that to be empty is to be nonexistent argue that existence must be intrinsic existence. This way of seeing things is natural. We see something cease. Our friend dies and we mourn. We are sad because we feel something intrinsically real has died. Thus seeing change makes us believe in intrinsic reality. Seeing things cease, we conclude that things must exist intrinsically.

Extending the debate, such an opponent might argue further that because things are produced, they must exist intrinsically. For, if they did not exist intrinsically, then nothing could be produced. Furthermore, they might argue, because things are annihilated or disintegrate, they must exist intrinsically. Moreover, she or he might claim, because things are permanent, they must exist intrinsically. Otherwise what would there be to exist permanently?

Furthermore, because things change they must exist intrinsically. We can see things moving away; without real things, there would be no movement, no change. Finally because things in relationship are either the same or different, things must exist intrinsically. Having these relationships of identity or distinctness presumes real entities. Otherwise there could not be relationships.

In order to refute these eight wrong views, Nāgārjuna presents the eight correct views, using their same logic, but turning their own logic back on the opponents. Hence Nāgārjuna presents these eight views in a manner diametrically opposed to the views of those who hold that some intrinsic reality exists. Nāgārjuna states that whatever is dependently originated has no intrinsic ceasing nor intrinsic production; no intrinsic annihilation and no intrinsic permanence; no intrinsic going nor intrinsic coming; and no intrinsic sameness nor intrinsic difference. In the subsequent twenty-seven chapters he explains these in vivid detail. Understanding emptiness of intrinsic existence means nothing more and nothing less than dependent origination.

Nāgārjuna thus refutes our intuitive way of understanding the world, a way that is often reified in philosophical traditions, including earlier Buddhist traditions. Tsongkhapa in *The Essence of Eloquent Interpretation* distinguishes two kinds of reification: innate reification and reification due to inept philosophy. While Nāgārjuna explicitly addresses the second, his real target is the first, innate reification.

Tsongkhapa presents the view condensing these eight characteristics of dependent origination into four pairs. The first pair of cessation and production relates to the nature of things. The second pair of disintegration and permanence relates to a temporal dimension. The third pair of coming and going relates to destination (spatial dimension). The fourth pair of sameness and difference relates to comparison between things. The first pair is about the things themselves; the main qualities of things are that they come into existence and are destroyed. This is why Nāgārjuna chose *production* and *cessation*. Moreover, things have duration; they last for some time. Thus there is permanence, in the sense of duration, followed at some point by disintegration. Furthermore, things have temporal-spatial locations. Due to having a spatial orientation, things come and go. Finally things are in relationship; things relate to other things through the qualities of sameness and diversity. This is how Buddhapālita explains the reason Nāgārjuna chose these particular eight characteristics to negate. It is also how he explains why Nāgārjuna chose just eight qualities of dependently originated phenomena to refute their intrinsic ontological status—and not more or less.

Yet another view of these eight characteristics relates to the experience of meditation on emptiness. Negation of these eight features from the perspective of meditation means the complete nonappearance of these eight extreme views during meditation. Thus Nāgārjuna is pointing to the most profound nonconceptual and nondual reality discovered through meditation: when the functionality of things (conventional reality) does not appear to the mind (of an unenlightened being). Realizing emptiness *directly* means without conceptual intermediaries. This makes the realization fresh, vibrant, penetrating, and transformative. So, while at the conventional level there are these eight extreme activities and characteristics, ultimately there are none of these. Freedom from these eight extremes is the meaning of emptiness of intrinsic nature.

## Emptiness Does Not Mean Nothingness

After we rise from the meditation on emptiness, intrinsic reality begins to fade. It takes on an illusory-like appearance. Previously, we thought there was an *I*, a *body*, and a *mind*, all of which convincingly appeared to exist objectively, from their own side. They actually appeared as though they were over there, or over here, as if we could point a finger at them. However, after prolonged meditation, nothing appears to exist anymore in the mode that it did before.

But is there still the feeling of a self after meditation? Some teachers say there will be the appearance of the body after meditation. Yet the body we previously believed to exist objectively no longer appears in the same way. We gain the conviction that the body is like an illusion; it is merely designated by our words and thoughts rather than existing intrinsically and objectively *over there*.

Take, for example, a house. Before we understand the emptiness of a house, we must acknowledge the reality of the perceived house. Everyone agrees there is a house. We can sleep in the house, we can eat in the house, and we can live in the house. Maybe there is a video of the house. The house is real. There has to be a house for there to be an empty house.

After we understand the emptiness of the house, what happens? The house itself does not disappear. The house remains, but our view of the house changes radically. Before understanding emptiness we viewed the house as existing objectively from its own side. Due to the house existing objectively it becomes an object of attachment or aversion. When we understand the idea of the intrinsically existent house is mistaken, then we understand the house to be merely designated by our mind. The more convinced we are in a merely designated house, the more our attachment declines.

Of course there is a basis of designation for the house: the physical combination of some walls, a door, a roof that forms the thing we call "house"—or any other thing, for that matter. But even this basis of designation does not exist intrinsically. The house is mentally created due to our preconceived ideas of a house. Therefore, when we conclude the house is empty, this does not mean that there is no house at all. It means there is no house like the intrinsically existent house we perceived before. We used to perceive the house existing intrinsically, independent of a perceiving mind. Even though *such* a house does not exist, still there does exist a house conventionally.

The existence of the conventionally existent house depends on the basis of designation, its name, and a mind that designates this name. When these three factors come together, then there is a conventionally existent house. Dependent origination means absence of independent existence. And absence of independent existence is precisely emptiness. Thus, *dependent origination* and *emptiness* have the same meaning.

## Emptiness and Dependent Origination

That emptiness and dependent origination have the same meaning is expressed elegantly in verses 18 and 19 of chapter 24 of *Fundamental Verses on the Middle Way*—two verses that capture the essence of Nāgārjuna's text:

18. **Whatever is dependently originated**
**is explained to be emptiness.**

That, being a dependent designation,
is itself the Middle Way.

19.  There does not exist anything
that is not dependently originated.
Therefore there does not exist
anything that is not empty.

Therefore, to understand emptiness correctly it is important to understand how things are fabricated by the mind.

Language and concepts are strong influences in our
reification of reality. Yet names and terms (designations)
have a basis. For example, let us consider the term *blue
flower*. To those people who have no understanding of
emptiness, blueness exists objectively, independent of
the mind designating the color blue. However, the existence of blue requires both a basis for this designation,
the mind designating the color blue, and the mental designation, blue, itself. To see something as blue is to label
it blue. Our color vocabulary determines how we carve
up the visible spectrum into colors, so that for some people two different frequencies will count as the same color
(blue) and for others they will not, depending on their
language and visual perception. This is a consequence
of nominalism about universals, and is a Buddhist position. Nothing intrinsic to the flower makes two instances of blueness instances of the same color. But nobody

could say that a color consists only in a name; animals can be taught to identify blueness without being taught language. And this is not to say that your typeface isn't blue, despite containing that name. Everything depends on other factors. Nothing exists alone. Everything exists in relationship to something else.

## Nuances of Dependence

There are three levels of dependent origination: (1) causal dependence; (2) dependence on parts and whole; and (3) dependence on terms and concepts (and designations).

The first is fairly easy to understand. We see effects arise in dependence on causes and conditions all the time.

Slightly subtler and more difficult to understand is dependence on parts and whole. From the Madhyamaka perspective, parts and whole are mutually dependent; you can't have one without the other. So without the wheels, axles, seat, and so on of a chariot (as illustrated by Candrakīrti), there is no chariot. Similarly, without the chariot, there are no parts: no wheels, axles, seat, and so on.

The subtlest dependent origination is dependence on names and concepts (and designations). From the Madhyamaka perspective, all phenomena depend not only on parts and whole and causes and conditions, but they also depend on designation. All things depend for their very identity on conceptual imputation. Since there is nothing existing from the side of the object, the only other ontological possibility is existence solely through conceptual imputation.

Dependence on designation has several aspects. In the Madhyamaka texts, three different analogies are presented when dependent designation is explained. Candrakīrti's analogy of a chariot is one.

In *Clear Words* Candrakīrti presents a different analogy: a story about mediation. In this story, two people visit a Hindu temple and see a painting of a deity on the wall. One says the painting depicts Iśvara, a Hindu entity sometimes synonymous with Śiva (called Wangchuk in Tibetan). The other person does not agree; he says the painting depicts Brahma. They argue. Then, in order to resolve their dispute, they seek help from the paṇḍita residing in that temple and ask him which of the two is correct. The wise man replies it is not Brahma; it is Iśvara. This story forms the basis for the analogy of one aspect of dependent designation: mediation, accepting what is true or agreed upon by worldly authority or convention. This is very important, as it demonstrates the fact that it is possible to distinguish truth and falsity within convention.

The Buddha said he does not debate with the world. Whatever is agreed upon by worldly convention to exist, he upholds. As he says in the *Chapter Teaching the Three Vows Sūtra* (*Trisaṃvaranirdeśaparivarta Sūtra*):

Ordinary people argue with me, but I do not argue
with them because whatever is asserted to be in the
world I also say exists. Whatever is asserted to be
nonexistent in the world I also say is nonexistent.[13]

Echoing these words of the Buddha, Candrakīrti in
*Entering the Middle Way* says this:

> Whatever it is—pot, cloth, tent, army, forest,
>     rosary, tree,
> House, small chariot, guest house, or any such
>     thing—
> You should know the conventions used by these
>     worldly beings.
> Why? Because the Master of Sages [the Buddha]
>     does not debate with the world.
> Part, quality, attachment, defining characteristic,
>     fuel, etc.,
> As well as whole, qualified, attached [person],
>     definienda, fire, etc.—These objects do not exist
>     in the seven ways under analysis like that applied
>     to the chariot.
> On the other hand, they do exist in terms of what is
>     familiar to the world.[14]

As Candrakīrti says earlier in the same text:

Just as things—pots and such—do not exist in reality,
But do exist in terms of what the world understands,
So it is for all things.[15]

Debating with worldly convention would throw out conventional truth, the second truth taught by the Buddha to be foundational in Buddhist epistemology. Rejecting conventional truth would be tantamount to nihilism. Nothing would make sense.

The third analogy for dependent origination is presented in Śāntideva's classic text, *A Guide to the Bodhisattva's Way of Life* (*Bodhicaryāvatāra*). Śāntideva gives us an example of an illusionist performing before a crowd. Using his magic, he creates the appearance of an illusionary elephant for all to see. The crowd buys into the appearance; they think it is a real elephant. The illusionist also sees the appearance of an elephant, but he knows it is not real, being merely created through his magic. A third person walking by looks, but he does not see the illusory elephant at all.

Here the illusionist is a metaphor for those who understand emptiness but still see the appearances of intrinsic existence; they see them, but they do not buy into them as real. This explains how apprehending deluded consciousness becomes saṁvṛti, a veil that conceals and obscures the truly empty nature of things. Things appear one way to our ordinary consciousness but exist in another. The passerby is a metaphor for an advanced practitioner completely immersed in nonconceptual wisdom of emptiness. We ordinary beings take illusion-like things to be intrinsically real, seeing the appearance and grasping on to it.

By applying these three analogies we come to the conclusion that things are, on the one hand, designated in dependence on the collection of their bases, and that, on the other hand, the designation is accepted without requiring deeper analysis. Furthermore, designation is accepted based on convention in accordance with what is known to the world, within a particular human (or possibly animal) linguistic community. Taken together, these three analogies illustrate how worldly conventional designation works.

## Does a Rope Snake Exist?

Not everything is accepted as conventionally true. Tsongkhapa explains that all conventionally existent things must meet three criteria to be valid phenomena and to be accepted as conventionally true. First, things must be known and accepted by worldly convention. Second, they must not be contradicted by other conventional valid cognitions known to the world. This criterion establishes accuracy of the convention. Third, they must not be contradicted by an analysis into ultimate reality.

When our mind perceives a snake where there is really a rope, the snake is a mere appearance. The Prāsaṅgikas agree with this. But when we perceive a real snake, designating its reality based upon the presence of its body and mind, this snake is also a mere appearance. At that level the two appearances have equal status; at that level they both are mere appearance. On the other hand, the rope-snake does not exist, even conventionally, whereas the snake imputed on the basis of its mind and body, does exist conventionally.

Geshé Akhu Sherap Gyatso[16] explained that the rope is the base upon which we mistakenly project a snake. But that base, the rope, is not a suitable or appropriate basis for the imputation of a snake, whereas a snake's body and mind *is* a suitable basis for its imputation. Yet a snake's body and mind is not identical with the snake, for reasons we have considered earlier.

Moreover, when we impute the existence of a snake on an appropriate basis, it cannot be undermined by other cognitions. A suitable basis is one that as soon as it appears, under normal circumstances, gives rise to an appropriate thought or projection. But a rope does not generate a perception of a snake unless there are unusual misleading circumstances, such as the approach of darkness or if the rope is coiled in a snake-like fashion.

Candrakīrti, in *Clear Words*, explains this through an analogy: If one attempts to make fire out of water, it is simply impossible. On the other hand if one attempts to make fire from wood, that of course is possible. Fire can be produced from wood. This means that water is not an appropriate or suitable condition or base for making fire. On the other hand wood is a suitable condition or base for making fire.

When our mind projects a chariot, the chariot is projected on the basis of its parts. There are the wheels, the nails, the wooden boards, the seats, and so forth. The chariot is just like an illusory elephant. It is merely an imputed appearance, and nothing more than that appearance. The parts are like the prop the magician uses to conjure it. What we have designated as a chariot does not intrinsically exist, as it appears covering its parts. The parts are in one sense a cause because without them a whole cannot be possible. However, on critical analysis cause and effect do not exist simultaneously. When there is wood and all the necessary prerequisites, then a result can be achieved, just like fire combusting from wood. Many things need to come together for the appearance of a chariot to arise.

## Becoming a Buddha

We must eliminate grasping at an intrinsic self in order to transform ourselves. We are able to shift our identity from our ordinary body and mind to the body and mind of a buddha. At first, this is accomplished using imagination in our meditation. Previously, our body was like the earth. The Buddha's wisdom body is like the sky. It seems impossible to transform this intrinsic solid body into a sky-like being. How can this big, solid earth transform into that spacious nonobstructing sky? While it may seem impossible, when we gain the conviction that we are merely designated and that an intrinsic self is mistaken, it becomes possible to shift our identity from something objective and solid to something nonobstructing and lacking intrinsic nature. This is the beginning of the process of cultivating an actual embodiment of buddhahood.

But, if we focus too much on the side of conventional reality, we may cling to it as intrinsically real. So once again we swing the pendulum toward seeing if conventional reality is really real.

# 1. The Twelve Links of Dependent Origination

## CHAPTER 26
### of Nāgārjuna's *Fundamental Verses on the Middle Way*

We begin our analysis of Nāgārjuna's *Fundamental Verses on the Middle Way* with chapter 26, "Analysis of the Twelve Links of Dependent Origination." This is the chapter with which Tsongkhapa, in the special insight section of his *Great Treatise on the Stages of the Path to Enlightenment*, starts one of his summaries of *Fundamental Verses on the Middle Way*, and where the Dalai Lama begins his own commentary on Nāgārjuna's great treatise. It begins with an account of dependent origination in terms of how we become trapped in this web of suffering we call life and concludes by showing how we can reverse that process to free ourselves.

All Buddhists accept dependent origination. Many non-Buddhists also accept a form of dependent origination that is especially prevalent in modern science and modern-day thinking. The Buddha's version is the twelve links of dependent origination, which explains the causal chain of how we are born and die repeatedly. He emphasized the dependent nature of our lives, which are fueled by an innate ignorance, which leads to aging and death. This explanation of the cycle of birth and death provides more detail into the second noble truth, the truth of the cause of suffering. It illustrates how we became trapped in this suffering existence, which cycles from one birth to another through the medium of a distorted ignorance of reality. It also gives us insight into how we can escape from this misery; the reverse process shows the path to enlightenment. Chapter 26, "Analysis of the Twelve Links of Dependent Origination," explains in detail how this process of confused saṃsāric existence takes place.

The twelve links of dependent origination actually function more like a spiral involving several lives, rather than a linear progression. A minimum of two lives and a maximum of three, most often not contiguous, are needed to complete one cycle. Nevertheless, the Buddha started his teaching with ignorance. Due to a distorted confusion, we grasp reality as if it had objective, intrinsic existence. In this way we reify reality. Due to clinging to such a reality, emotional responses of attraction or aversion are elicited. We become attached and angry, and we generate the many permutations of these emotions. Acting on these emotions born from ignorance, we think we are making ourselves happy. But in actuality we are just creating the causes for more suffering.

Gaining insight into the sequence of events that creates suffering gives us insight into how to disrupt it. Through analyzing ignorance and cultivating its counterforce, the wisdom of realizing emptiness, we reverse this misery and become free from suffering. Thus, through understanding chapter 26, "Analysis of the Twelve Links of Dependent Origination," we develop the special insight that realizes emptiness, which is the method, as well as the door, to get out.

### *Root Verses of Chapter 26*

1. Obscured by ignorance we perform the three types of action [positive, negative, unwavering]. These actions create birth that propels us through further transmigration.

2. Having actions as its conditions, consciousness enters transmigration. Once consciousness has entered, then name and form develop.

3. Once name and form develop, the six sense spheres arise.

Depending on the six sense spheres,
contact will then arise.

4. Contact arises only in dependence
on the eye, form, and apprehension.
Thus dependent upon name and form,
consciousness arises.

5. From the meeting of the three—
eye, form, and consciousness—
contact will then arise,
and from contact feeling will arise.

6. Dependent on feeling is craving;
one craves because of feeling.
Craving strengthens into grasping,
maturing the four types of grasping.

7. When nourished by grasping,
[future] existence fully matures.
Without grasping there is freedom
from further [cyclic] existence.

8. Existence also is the five aggregates.
From existence arises birth. From birth, certainly
will arise aging, death, grieving, lamentation,
mental anguish, distress, and suffering.

9. Likewise mental anguish and distress
arise from [unenlightened] birth.
Thus what arises is merely
a great mass of suffering.

10. The root of cyclic existence is action;
therefore the wise do not act.
The unwise become agents,
whereas the wise see reality.

11. With the cessation of ignorance,
actions cease to arise.
Ignorance ceases through insight
and meditation on suchness.

12. Through the cessation of these,
those will not manifest.
In this way the entire mass
of suffering completely ceases.

The first verse of this chapter introduces the schema
for the twelve links of interdependent origination, stating
that from ignorance (the first link) is produced the delusions, which in turn produce karma or action (the second
link), which then propels cyclic existence and all the layers of suffering it entails. That is, covered by the darkness
of ignorance, we take rebirth.

The second verse further elaborates this process of cyclic existence. Karmic seeds or imprints (Skt. *bīja*; Tib. *bag chags*) are deposited on the stream of consciousness. Consciousness (the third link) enters into the next life. At the beginning of the next life, consciousness becomes a cooperative cause for the creation of name and form (the fourth link). "Name and form" refers to the five aggregates: our body and different aspects of our consciousness. The first aggregate is material form, which refers to our body. The remaining four aggregates are feelings, discriminations, compositional factors, and consciousness. These are collectively called "name."

Once name and form come into being, the six sense spheres (the fifth link, these are the eyes, ears, and so forth) are produced. Thereby the sense of touch is produced, as explained in the third verse. Dependent on name and form and the sense of touch, rebirth takes place. The sense of touch represents sensory consciousness. Therefore, the meaning is that our ordinary consciousness is produced depending on the five aggregates.

Above, we saw that consciousness in general is the cooperative cause for the five aggregates. In this context, we see that each of the specific sensory consciousnesses is produced from the five aggregates. This is explained as follows: from form, sensory cognition and composed phenomena, the fifth aggregate of sensory consciousness, is produced. *Form* here refers to the five sense faculties.

Sensory cognition comprises the five sensory conscious-nesses associated with those five sense faculties. *Composed phenomena* here refers to contact with a tangible object. Thus, when the sense faculties come into contact with their objects, the corresponding sense consciousnesses are produced. This is the further explanation of dependent origination presented in the fourth verse.

The meeting of these three—sense faculties such as the tactile faculty, the sensory objects such as tangible form, and the tactile sensory consciousnesses—creates contact (the sixth link); this is the subject of the fifth verse. From contact, sensation (the seventh link) is produced.

Feeling, or sensation, produces craving (the eighth link), which strengthens to grasping (the ninth link). The sequence of these three links—seven, eight, and nine—is explained in the sixth verse.

Grasping produces existence (the tenth link), the last karma for one lifetime. It takes a minimum of two and a maximum of three lifetimes to complete one cycle of the twelve dependent links. The subsequent lifetimes are not necessarily contiguous; indeed, they usually are not. In fact, it is often the case that many lifetimes intervene before one cycle of twelve interdependent links is complet-ed. This suggests that we have countless incomplete cycles of the twelve interdependent links awaiting completion.[17]

In the first two lines of the seventh verse, we see how grasping matures into a new existence (the ninth link), followed by birth (the tenth link), thus sustaining cyclic existence. The last two lines explain the interruption of cyclic existence. By stopping grasping, freedom from cyclic existence is attained.

Existence and birth manifest in the body and mind, which are the five aggregates. These five aggregates are permated by suffering. Suffering is the result of delusion and karma. It consists of aging, death, sorrow, weeping, and misery. This further unfolding of the miserable state of affairs of cyclic existence is explained in the eighth verse.

Great disturbances to our emotional and physical lives are produced from craving and grasping. Thus, from ignorance, craving, and grasping, the suffering of the unsatisfactory aggregates is produced. The ninth verse presents the result of this cycle, that the interdependently originated twelve links are simply a mass of great suffering.

Karma based on ignorance propels us into saṃsāra. Acting out of the ignorance of not knowing reality unwittingly creates problems. Therefore, the wise do not create negative karma. Verse 10 demonstrates the paths to bondage and to freedom.

When ignorance is brought to an end, action (karma) no longer arises. Ignorance is brought to an end through understanding and meditating on emptiness. Thus, the cessation of ignorance, and with it the complete chain of suffering, is accomplished through the understanding of emptiness. The eleventh verse explains the end of ignorance and thereby the end of suffering.

When the cause of saṃsāra ceases, all the subsequent links no longer arise. This is somewhat analogous to the domino effect, though in dominoes, when one falls, all the others fall in sequence; here the twelve links may fall all at once when their original cause (ignorance) has been eliminated. No further effort or action is required once ignorance is eliminated, as the succeeding links will naturally no longer arise. In this way the continuity of suffering—contaminated aggregates—is exhausted. Unenlightened existence finally comes to an end.

# 2. The Self

CHAPTER 18

of Nāgārjuna's *Fundamental Verses*
*on the Middle Way*

When the Dalai Lama teaches Nāgārjuna's *Fundamental Verses on the Middle Way*, after explaining chapter 26, "Analysis of the Twelve Links of Dependent Origination," he then turns to chapter 18, "Analysis of the Self." This is the only chapter of all the twenty-seven chapters in the text where Nāgārjuna focuses primarily on the selflessness of the person. Having learned how we get trapped in this confused saṃsāric existence in chapter 26, we have a tendency to grasp at the confused self as real. To push back against this tendency, here, in chapter 18, Nāgārguna moves the pendulum back to selflessness.

*Root Verses of Chapter 18*

1. **If the self were the aggregates,**
**it would have to arise and disintegrate.**

If the self were different from the aggregates,
it would not have the characteristics of the
    aggregates.

2. Thus if there were no self,
how could there be mine?
Because both self and mine are pacified,
there is no more grasping to "I" and "mine."

3. The one not grasping at "I" and "mine"
also does not exist [intrinsically].
Whoever sees one without grasping at 'I' and 'mine'
as intrinsically existent does not see [ultimate
    reality].

4. When thoughts of "I" and "mine" extinguish
with respect to the inner or outer [analyzing self
    among or apart from aggregates],
the appropriated ceases.
As it ceases, so does birth.

5. Elimination of karma and delusion leads to
    nirvāṇa.
Karma and delusion arise from conceptualization.
Conceptualization arises from mental
    elaboration.
Mental elaboration ceases through emptiness.

6. The buddhas taught there is a self.
The buddhas also taught there is no self.
They have further taught there is
neither self nor no self.

7. What language expresses is repudiated,
because the object of mind is repudiated.
Unborn and unceasing like nirvāṇa,
such is the suchness of things.

8. Everything is real, and is not real,
both real and not real,
neither real nor not real.
This is Lord Buddha's teaching.

9. Not known from others' words, free,
not fabricated by mental elaboration,
not conceptualized, nor differentiated.
This characterizes suchness.

10. Whatever arises in dependence on
another is not [intrinsically] identical,
nor is it [intrinsically] different, thus it is
neither nonexistent nor eternal.

11. This is the nectar, the doctrine
of the buddhas, saviors of the world.

Without identity, without difference,
neither nonexistent nor eternal.

12. When the fully enlightened buddhas do not
    appear,
and even the śrāvakas have disappeared,
the wisdom of the self-enlightened ones
will arise completely without reliance on others.

Teachings on the twelve links of dependent origination are common to all Buddhist schools, but the interpretation of dependent origination varies among them.
This is especially true of the first link: ignorance.

The Madhyamaka school understands ignorance dif-
ferently from all other philosophical schools. Accordingly, their view of emptiness, the negation of the object of
ignorance, also varies. The other schools define ignorance
as grasping at a substantially autonomous self or person.
This self is understood by them to be separate from the
aggregates and relates to them like a master ruling over
the body and mind. This self is said to be self-sufficient
and substantially real. For the non-Madhyamaka schools,
to negate this self, which is distinct from the aggregates,
is to realize selflessness. So for them, ignorance is grasping
at this self-sufficient, substantially autonomous self.

Nāgārjuna argues that this does not reach the subtlest
meaning of selflessness, because this leaves grasping at the

*aggregates*—that into which the self is decomposed by analysis—untouched, and to take them to exist intrinsically is a deeper form of ignorance. His *Precious Garland* states this:

> As long as one grasps the aggregates,
> there is indeed a sense of "I."
> When there is a sense of "I," there again is action
> (karma).
> From that, there is again birth.[18]

According to Nāgārjuna, ignorance is not only grasping at an intrinsically existent *self* but also grasping at intrinsically existent *phenomena*. The five aggregates include all phenomena; that is, material form and consciousness. Thus, for Mādhyamikas there are two loci of emptiness to realize: the emptiness of the self and the emptiness of phenomena. Emptiness is the same in both cases, but the basis for emptiness varies. In order to comprehend the subtlest aspect of ignorance, Nāgārjuna argues that we must understand not only the emptiness of the self but also the emptiness of phenomena.

The Dalai Lama writes in *The Middle Way* that the search for the nature of the self, which does not want suffering and does want peace and happiness, may have begun somewhere around three thousand years ago. He discusses hypothetically how people a long time ago might have pondered about the nature of this self. For instance, they may have asked, "where is this self located?" They might have concluded that the self is wherever you are. This is a way of understanding what it is to take oneself as the center of the universe, a tendency we all recognize both as an innate cognitive reflex and as fundamentally irrational. From this deep instinctual feeling and identity that "I am," they might have concluded there is an enduring thing like a real self. This belief in a real self, independent from the aggregates, seems to have been common before the advent of the Buddha. It is also a common belief today among most people who are not Buddhists or Jains.

In this chapter, Nāgārjuna goes into more detail about knowing and not knowing reality accurately. He explains emptiness from the deeper perspective of its characteristics or nature, its purpose, and its meaning. He claims that those who reify reality are committed to understanding existence as intrinsic existence because they do not appreciate emptiness. Although they say they accept dependent origination, in fact, they use it to once again hold onto intrinsic existence. Therefore, Nāgārjuna says that they do not appreciate the subtleties of reality. Moreover, Nāgārjuna argues, they do not comprehend the purpose of realizing emptiness. Finally, he says that those who reify reality do not understand the meaning or outcome of having studied and understood emptiness.

These reasons may have lead Nāgārjuna to write this chapter, "Analysis of the Self." The term *self* has two meanings in Buddhism. First, it refers to a person, or, in this sense, any being having a mind. Hence *person*, or *self*, refers to both humans and nonhuman living beings. Second, *self* in the context of self-existence means existence from the side of the object, or intrinsic existence. In Sanskrit, this is called *prapañca*, which actually means *fabrication*. To grasp the self in this way is to take all existence to be objective and independent from the perceiving and conceiving mind.

This mode of misunderstanding existence is precisely what is meant by *ignorance*. This ignorance binds us to the unsatisfactory state of saṃsāra. This cycling of birth and death is fraught with misery at every turn; even the only occasional respites are just suffering in disguise. Understanding this is the key to renunciation, which leads to freedom from suffering. Therefore, analyzing the self will lead to the absence of an intrinsic self, and seeing beyond it utilizing the wisdom of realizing emptiness is the result of such an analysis.

If the self were the same as the aggregates, as the aggregates arise and disintegrate, the self also would have to arise and disintegrate. Tsongkhapa, in the special insight section of *The Great Treatise on the Stages of the Path to Enlightenment*, presents six fallacies arising from the position of identity between the self and the aggregates:

There would be six fallacies: it would be pointless to assert a self; there would be many selves; object and agent would be one; actions that were performed would perish; the effects of actions not done would be encountered; and the statements by the Buddha about remembering past lives would be invalid. So do not assert that the self and the aggregates are one.[19]

If the self were separate from the aggregates, it could not possess the characteristics of the aggregates. Therefore, the self cannot exist intrinsically. This is how this chapter opens, proving that the self can be neither identical nor different from the aggregates. As there is no third possibility, such a self cannot exist. It is this first verse of chapter 18 that evoked in Tsongkhapa his first direct realization of emptiness, free of any conceptual intermediaries. Accordingly, this first verse is a pith instruction.

If the self does not exist intrinsically, then the things that belong to the self also do not exist intrinsically. Realizing the "I" and "mine" not to exist intrinsically naturally leads to the relinquishing of grasping at an "I" and a "mine." This is the reasoning set forth in the second verse.

Furthermore, meditators who abandon grasping the reality of the self or self-possession do not intrinsically exist either; not only is there no intrinsically existent self, there is also no intrinsically existent person to perceive such an intrinsically existent self.

Those who reify reality demand that there must be a person, for it is the person who eliminates the self-grasping mind. This is the argument presented in the third verse by those who reify reality. The Prāsaṅgikas reiterate that there is no intrinsically existent person who eliminates the self-grasping mind. Moreover, as there is no intrinsically existent self, this allows for abandoning bondage in cyclic existence. The fourth verse recalls the argument that it is precisely the lack of intrinsic existence that allows the possibility of attaining freedom from suffering.

The elimination of karma and delusion occurs with the elimination of all self-grasping minds, which will gradually disappear with the realization of emptiness. When karma and delusion are completely abandoned, nirvāṇa automatically is attained. This self-grasping mind distorts reality. All of these mistaken appearances will be eliminated through understanding emptiness. The fifth verse emphasizes the role the wisdom of realizing emptiness plays in attaining nirvāṇa through the elimination of ignorance and the self-grasping mind that generates mistaken appearances.

An alternative reading of this verse involves reading each line as parameterized, either as conventional or ultimate. Conventionally there is a self; ultimately there is not. Conventionally there is a self and ultimately there is not a self; neither is there an ultimate self, nor is there not a conventional self. This is the meaning of the sixth verse.

When the emptiness of all phenomena is nonconceptually (directly) realized, then all varieties of reified concepts—those created out of language, those using words, and those crystalized as thoughts—will disappear. When the mind equipoises in a state of emptiness nonconceptually, or views all phenomena as illusory, this impedes the arising of self-grasping. From this, we can understand the possibility of the complete cessation of self-grasping. This is what is expressed in the seventh verse.

The Buddha sometimes taught that things exist truly. Yet on other occasions he taught that nothing exists truly. For the sake of beings of lesser intelligence the Buddha taught that things exist truly. For the sake of beings of higher intelligence he taught that nothing exists truly. This was done in order to guide beings of lesser intelligence along the path. When they were mature enough and had the capacity to understand, then the Buddha would teach them the view of no self. This is the method of *upāya*, "expedient means" or "pedagogy." The eighth verse explains the reasons why the Buddha sometimes taught there is a self and sometimes taught there is no self.

Things not truly existent have the capacity to change. Birth and death illustrate change. So changing things cannot exist intrinsically. Even ultimate truth, the absence of intrinsic existence, does not exist intrinsically. Worldly wisdom that does not engage in the ultimate nature of reality cannot realize emptiness. This emptiness is not known from others' words, naturally free from intrinsicality, beyond fabrication, without conceptuality, and not separate. This nonseparateness from the perspective of emptiness applies to all phenomena equally (even emptiness itself). It means from the perspective of being empty of intrinsic existence, all phenomena are the same without even one iota of difference. They become like water poured into water. These are the five characteristics of ultimate truth explained in the ninth verse. Illustrating this further, in his book *Engaging Buddhism*, Jay Garfield recalls the words of Dōgen, the early thirteenth-century founder of the Sōtō school of Zen Buddhism:

> Dōgen wrote that "to study the self is to forget the self; to forget the self is to be affirmed by myriad things. When actualized by myriad things, your body and mind as well as the bodies and minds of others drop away" (Tanahashi 1985, 72). . . . The more we pay attention honestly to our own nature, the more we realize that there is no such nature; the more we pay attention to our own subjective character, the more we realize that we are not subjects; the more we realize that, the more we realize that that to which we respond as *our* object is not apprehended as it is; and the more we can shed the myth of subject-object duality and the immediacy of our relation to subjectivity, the more honestly we can understand our participation in

the reality we inhabit. This is the goal of a Buddhist phenomenology.

I close this with a poem of Dōgen:

> Being in the world.
> To what can it be compared?
> Dwelling in a dewdrop,
> Fallen from a waterfowl's beak,
> The image of the moon.
> (quoted in Kasulis 1981, 103)

Note that here there is no focus on subjectivity, no focus on the character of experience, only of an ephemeral, impermanent, impersonal existence pregnant with illusion, but also with beauty.[20]

Not only impermanent things, but also things produced in dependence on other things are incapable of existing intrinsically. It follows that this is true of emptiness itself; emptiness itself also lacks intrinsic existence. Therefore, a proper understanding of emptiness is free from reification. Moreover, emptiness is a quality of all things, including emptiness. Thus to see things as empty is to be free from nihilism. Because emptiness induces dependent production, which is another reason the view of emptiness is free from nihilism. These arguments demonstrating how emptiness is free from the two extremes of nihilism and reification are presented in the tenth verse.

This teaching is like nectar. There is no sameness in the nature of emptiness. There is no difference in the nature of emptiness. The eleventh verse reinforces this essential understanding of emptiness being free from the two extreme views.

When the Buddha is absent from this world and his disciples have disappeared from this world, then self-realizing arhats (pratyekabuddhas) will come to meditate on emptiness. Their wisdom will be produced solely from their understanding emptiness, without the need for a teacher. Solace that the teachings and the realizations will continue, even in the absence of the buddhas, is presented in the twelfth verse.

# 3. The Four Noble Truths

## CHAPTER 24
## of Nāgārjuna's *Fundamental Verses on the Middle Way*

In the chapters previous to this one, Nāgārjuna relentlessly challenges many notions of intrinsic existence. He does this so exhaustively that some might misinterpret his arguments to mean that nothing exists. Then they might think that since nothing exists, everyone can do whatever they want, for nothing really matters. This would be a grave error not only for the individual but also for society in general.

Tsongkhapa and other great scholars say it is relatively easy to see the nonfindability of things, but it is much harder to understand emptiness. Understanding of emptiness abides free from the two extremes of reification and nihilism. For this reason this chapter is pivotal—some even consider it to be the most important chapter in *Fundamental Verses on the Middle Way*. This is why, after discussing emptiness in great detail in chapter 18, "Analysis of the Self," the Dalai Lama teaches chapter 24, "Analysis of the Four Noble Truths."

When the Dalai Lama teaches this chapter, he extracts layers of meaning of the four noble truths from the perspective of their characteristics (or nature), functions, and outcomes, which are eventually experienced through direct realization. This dovetails well with the main structure of Buddhist practice—the ground, path, and result. The understanding of the nature of reality is the ground. The path is pursued based on an understanding of the ground. Finally, the result is experienced as an effect of cultivating the path. Another way this is taught is as follows: The ground is reality, which is the two truths. The path is the two accumulations of merit and wisdom. The result is the union of the two bodies of a buddha: the form body and the truth body.[21]

This chapter is the heart of Nāgārjuna's treatise.

### Root Verses of Chapter 24

1. If all of this is empty then there is
no arising and no disintegrating.
For you, then it would absurdly follow that
the four noble truths do not exist.

2. If the four noble truths do not exist,
then complete understanding, abandonment,

cultivation, and actualization
would not be possible.

3.  If these things do not exist,
the four fruits cannot exist. Without fruits,
there are no [four] attainers of these fruits,
and hence no [four] enterers into
     [the paths].

4.  If there were no eight kinds of persons[22]
     [four attainers and four enterers]
there would be no Saṅgha;
and since the four noble truths do not exist,
the exalted Dharma would also not exist.

5.  If there is no Dharma and no Saṅgha,
how could there be a Buddha?
If emptiness is presented in this way, it
undermines the Three Precious Jewels.

6.  It also undermines everything:
the existence of the fruits,
distinguishing moral from immoral action,
and all worldly conventions.

7.  You who speak this way have failed
to understand the purpose of emptiness,

emptiness itself, and the meaning of emptiness.
Therefore you are harmed by it.

8.  The teachings given by all the buddhas
are founded perfectly on two truths:
the truth of worldly convention
and the ultimate truth.

9.  Those who do not properly understand
the distinction between these
two truths do not properly understand
the buddhas' profound teachings on suchness.

10.  Without a basis of conventional truth,
the ultimate truth cannot be taught.
Without understanding the ultimate,
nirvāṇa cannot be attained.

11.  Through misunderstanding emptiness
a person of little intelligence is destroyed;
just like a snake wrongly seized,
or a magic spell wrongly cast.

12.  Hence the Buddha's intention to teach
the profound Dharma was silenced,
knowing how difficult it is to penetrate
the depths of this profound teaching.

13. Since your erroneous objections
are not relevant to emptiness,
your rejection of emptiness
is not relevant to me.

14. To whom emptiness makes sense
everything makes sense.
To whom emptiness does not make sense
nothing makes sense.

15. When you fully impose
on me all of your own faults,
you are like a man riding his horse
who has forgotten where his horse is.

16. When you view the existence of things
solely in terms of intrinsic nature,
then you view things devoid
of their causes and conditions.

17. Effects and their causes;
agent, action, and object;
arising and disintegration:
you thereby reject all these as well.

18. Whatever is dependently originated
is explained to be emptiness.

That, being a dependent designation,
is itself the Middle Way.

19.  There does not exist anything
that is not dependently originated.
Therefore there does not exist
anything that is not empty.

20.  If all of this is not empty there would
be neither arising nor disintegration.
Thus it would follow for you that
the four noble truths would not exist.

21.  If things were not dependently originated,
how could suffering come to be?
That which is impermanent is spoken of as
        suffering [by the Buddha].
This does not apply to intrinsic existence.

22.  If things existed intrinsically,
how could anything thoroughly arise?
Thus for he who combats emptiness
there is no origin [of suffering].

23.  If suffering existed intrinsically,
cessation would not exist.
Intrinsic existence denotes existing forever.
Therefore, it undermines cessation.

24. If the path existed intrinsically,
there could be no meditation.
But since the path is meditated upon,
your intrinsic nature cannot exist.

25. If suffering, its origin, and
its cessation are nonexistent,
which cessation of suffering [attained]
by the path is posited by you?

26. By its [truth of suffering] intrinsic nature,
if it is not thoroughly understood [earlier],
how could it be thoroughly apprehended [later];
doesn't it exist intrinsically?

27. Just as with your understanding,
your abandonment, actualization,
cultivation, and the four fruits
would have no meaning.

28. For you espousing intrinsic nature,
the fruits would already be realized
just because of their intrinsic nature.
Therefore what is to be realized?

29. Without the fruits no one could attain them.
Thus there could not be enterers as well.

And without the eight kinds of persons,
there would be no Saṅgha.

30.  If the four noble truths do not exist,
the precious Dharma would not exist.
If the Dharma and Saṅgha do not exist,
then how could there be a Buddha?

31.  In your view a Buddha would absurdly
not depend upon enlightenment.
And enlightenment would absurdly
not depend upon a Buddha.

32.  Because of your [view] of intrinsic existence,
the one who is not enlightened,
even if the deeds of enlightenment are pursued,
will never achieve enlightenment.

33.  No one could ever perform
moral or immoral actions if things
were not empty, for intrinsic nature
precludes all activity whatsoever.

34.  For you without virtue or nonvirtue,
results would ensue.
[Thus] for you effects that arise
from virtuous and nonvirtuous causes do not exist.

35.  If for you effects coming from
moral and immoral causes did exist,
then why are these effects arising from
moral and immoral causes not empty?

36.  He who combats this emptiness,
which is dependent origination,
undermines all the worldly
conventions [as well].

37.  For if emptiness itself is violated,
nothing could function at all.
[Hence] there would be actions without
agents and agents without actions.

38.  If there were intrinsic existence transmigrators
would never arise, nor would they ever disintegrate
and would last forever,
absent of multiplicity of situations.

39.  If things were not empty,
the unattained could not be attained,
karma and afflictions could not be eliminated,
also, delusions in their entirety could be
eliminated.

40. But whoever sees dependent origination
also sees [the truth of] suffering,
its origin and its cessation,
and the path [to cessation].

The twenty-fourth chapter opens by laying out, in the first six verses, the primary objections to the view that everything is empty, from those who take existence to be inherent existence.

In the first verse, those who reify reality put forward their strong counterproposal, which is based on a misunderstanding of the meaning of intrinsic existence. The Prāsaṅgikas reject all intrinsic existence based primarily on the view of dependent origination, and the proponents of intrinsic existence claim that if things were indeed empty of intrinsic existence, as the Prāsaṅgikas say, then nothing could be produced and nothing could cease. Therefore, cause-and-effect relationships would not be tenable. Hence nothing would exist. This would include the four noble truths, which consist of a pair of cause-and-effect relationships: suffering and its cause, and liberation and its cause. Since cause-and-effect relationships do not exist, it would follow that the four noble truths do not exist.

The third and fourth verses discuss the four achievements (stream-enterer, once-returner, nonreturner, and ārhat) and the four enterers into achievement.

The following twelve elaborations repeat the four noble truths from different perspectives that dive deeper. The first repetition is *identifying* (sometimes called *nature*) the four noble truths: (1) *this is* suffering as seen through the wisdom eyes of āryas; (2) *this is* the cause of suffering as seen through the wisdom eyes of āryas; (3) *this is* the cessation of suffering as seen through the wisdom eyes of āryas; (4) *this is* the path leading to the cessation of suffering as seen through the wisdom eyes of āryas. The second repetition is the action we take to make these four noble truths part of our being (sometimes called *function*) and is where we adopt the four achievements: (5) *know* the suffering; (6) *abandon* the origin; (7) *cultivate* the path; (8) *actualize* the cessation. The third repetition is the wisdom that results as part of our experience: (9) suffering is to be known, but there is *nothing to be known*; (10) the origin is to be abandoned, but there is *nothing to abandon*; (11) the path is to be cultivated, but there is *nothing to cultivate*; (12) cessation is to be actualized, but there is *nothing to actualize*.

Those nearly achieving these attainments are like those who have entered the stream of liberation by realizing reality. Further purification leads one to coming back for one more life (or several lifetimes) to complete the work. This discussion hinges on whether these eight achievements and enterers exist intrinsically or not. The argument from those who reify reality is this: if things did not exist intrinsically, then the four achievements and the four entries into these achievements would not exist. Therefore, they conclude that things must exist intrinsically. The Prāsaṅgikas reverse this argument—a style of debate that is familiar, as it recurs in Nāgārjuna's strategy. Their rebuttal: if things did exist intrinsically, then these four achievements and the four entries into these four achievements would not be possible. Then it would be those who reify reality, and not the Prāsaṅgikas, who would face such consequences.

In the second verse, those who reify reality continue their defense of intrinsic existence, arguing that if there were no intrinsic existence, then none of the ways of approaching the four noble truths would be possible. The four ways of approaching the four noble truths are complete understanding (the truth of suffering), abandonment (the truth of the cause of suffering), cultivation (the truth of the path), and actualization (the truth of cessation). If the four noble truths did not exist, then there could be no complete understanding, abandonment, cultivation, and actualization. Therefore, there would be no one trying to eliminate the first two truths and accomplish the last two truths. If the four noble truths did not exist, the four achievements would not be possible.

Ignorance gives rise to delusions, which in turn give rise to karma. Karma in turn gives rise to suffering. Suffering has causes, which makes it possible to remove them, and hence the suffering itself. The complete elimination of ignorance, karma, and delusion is liberation. The truth of cessation is the Dharma. The one who actualizes Dharma in its entirety is a buddha. Those who have nonconceptually realized emptiness are the saṅgha. Thus, if the Dharma did not exist, nor would a buddha, nor would the saṅgha. These are the further consequences of misunderstanding the teaching of no intrinsic existence by those who reify reality, as presented in the third verse.

Thus the eight kinds of arhats often mentioned in the sūtras would not exist. Therefore, there would be no saṅgha. If there were no saṅgha, then there would be no truth of the ārya saṅgha. Hence there would be no Dharma. In this fourth verse, those who reify reality continue drawing out consequences based on their lack of understanding of intrinsic existence, concluding at this point that there would be no Dharma.

If there were no saṅgha and no Dharma, then how could there be a buddha? Therefore, the Prāsaṅgika's position that holds everything to be empty would consequently reject the most precious Three Jewels. In the fifth verse, those who reify reality conclude that there would be no precious Triple Gem in the absence of intrinsic existence.

Not only would rejection of intrinsic existence damage the four fruits, it would also undermine all nonvirtues and all virtues. Thus, all conventional phenomena would cease to exist. In this way there would be no world and no beings inhabiting this nonexistent world. This is the further consequence of no intrinsic existence from the perspective of those who reify reality, as presented in the sixth verse.

In the seventh verse, Nāgārjuna responds. From the first to the sixth verse, those who reify reality presented the full consequences of no intrinsic existence as they see it. Those who think that to exist is to be nonempty and to be empty is to be nonexistent have no understanding of the purpose of emptiness. Nor do they appreciate the cultivation and achievement of the understanding of emptiness. Furthermore, those who reify reality have no understanding of the meaning of emptiness.

Due to this misunderstanding, those who reify reality misinterpret the Prāsaṅgika position to be a view that rejects the existence of everything. The irony of this is about to come; Nāgārjuna is about to turn the tables, charging the reificationist himself with nihilism.

The teachings of the Buddha comprise the two truths: the conventional truth and the ultimate truth. This understanding of reality represents a deeper level of the Buddha's teachings. The things with which we engage in everyday life do exist in the framework of one and do not in the framework of the other. But we need one to explain and to reach the other. This is very important, because here Nāgārjuna distinguishes them and tells us that we need to understand that distinction in order to avoid the extremes of nihilism and reification. Yet in the eighteenth verse Nāgārjuna tells us that they are inseparable and that we need to understand that inseparability to avoid those very extremes.

From our understanding of the two truths, we're able to comprehend the four noble truths, the bedrock of the Buddha's teachings. Recognizing there are causes to our suffering allows for the possibility of eliminating suffering; the four noble truths are a guide leading us out of suffering. This path leads to the total cessation of suffering. Thus, the conventional leads us to the ultimate. And without the ultimate there could be no conventional. The conventional relies on relationships like cause and effect, which are only made possible by ultimate emptiness. Extending the cessation of suffering to all living beings then summarizes the essence of the Buddha's teachings of universal unconditioned compassion—bodhicitta. This is presented in the eighth verse.

Those who do not understand these two truths have no understanding of the essence of the Buddha's teachings. This reiteration of the importance of the two truths is reconfirmed in the ninth verse.

Without depending on the conventional truth one cannot understand the ultimate truth. Moreover, without understanding ultimate truth one cannot attain nirvāṇa. This tenth verse is important because it emphasizes the importance of conventional truth and the need to not disparage it. We cannot just go straight to the ultimate. It must be realized by careful understanding that can only be achieved through language, conceptual thought, and a thorough engagement with conventional reality, which is the basis of emptiness. And in order to understand conventional reality, we need to understand emptiness. Each supports the other—they are, in fact, nondually related.

This tenth verse has an important relationship with the eighteenth verse. Verse 10 presents the important distinction between the two truths. In verse 18, we find the explanation of the identity of the two truths. Thus, both are important verses to fully comprehend.

> Emptiness is not the annihilation of convention, but
> the ability to return to convention, seeing it merely as
> conventional. Discursive thought returns; language
> is again used, but now understood merely as a tool,
> not as a mirror of reality itself.[23]

This intimate and quintessential connection between conventional truth, ultimate truth, and attaining nirvāṇa is presented here in the tenth verse, as well as in the eighteenth verse. Both are necessary for avoiding the two extremes.

If one does not know how to understand emptiness correctly, then those with less intelligence will be lost. The eleventh verse presents two analogies illustrating the potential disastrous consequences of misunderstanding emptiness. In the first analogy, the danger that exists in misunderstanding emptiness is described to be like the danger of a beginner without proper training trying to catch a poisonous snake. In the second analogy, this danger is the same as an untrained beginner, without knowing the proper technique, attempting to cast a spell using black magic. Using the first example, a poisonous snake can be very beneficial if grasped properly, since its venom can have medicinal value. But if grasped improperly, it kills the grasper. The analogy therefore runs deep. Grasp emptiness properly and you become free. Grasp it improperly and your suffering is never ending. This is particularly relevant when the two truths are not understood and one thereby concludes that emptiness itself exists in some absolute way—this grave misunderstanding is very difficult to correct.

For these reasons the Buddha fully understood how difficult it would be for those with immature wisdom to understand the profound reality correctly. Therefore, he remained silent and did not teach for some time after attaining enlightenment; this is explained in the twelfth verse.

The very same arguments those who think that to exist is to be nonempty and to be empty is to be nonexistent have used to refute the Prāsaṅgikas are now turned upon the reificationists.

The Prāsaṅgikas claim they are immune to the consequences presented by those who reify reality. Moreover, those who reify reality must now face these same consequences they tried to force on the Prāsaṅgikas. In the thirteenth verse, due to a fundamental misunderstanding of emptiness, the faults thrust on the Prāsaṅgikas are now turned back onto the reificationists in a bit of philosophical jujitsu. Nāgārjuna is charging the opponent who thinks Nāgārjuna is a nihilist with being that very thing himself.

The fourteenth verse presents the well-known classic position of the Prāsaṅgikas:

14. To whom emptiness makes sense
everything makes sense.
To whom emptiness does not make sense
nothing makes sense.

This verse has sometimes been used to summarize the Prāsaṅgika view of reality. It particularly emphasizes the conventional truth, demonstrating the functionality of emptiness. This verse demonstrates how reality is able to function despite all phenomena lacking intrinsic existence.

Those who reify reality are accused of mistakenly transferring their own faults onto the Prāsaṅgikas. Verse 15 compares this to a person riding a horse who forgets he is on a horse. The horseback rider is riding around his property counting his horses: 1, 2, and 3. He knows he had a fourth horse yesterday. So he accuses another person of having stolen one of his horses, as the other person is riding a horse that looks a lot like the one he can't find. The other person points out that in fact the rider forgot to count the horse he is riding. Thus, the rider accuses the other person of riding the horse that in fact he is riding. The opponent accuses Nāgārjuna of riding the dark horse of nihilism, when in fact he is riding it himself.

The sixteenth verse informs us that actually the opposite is true. When those who reify reality view everything existing intrinsically, in fact they are rejecting everything. Reification precludes relations. Relations mean dependence. Reification views everything as intrinsic or independent. Whatever exists independently, by definition, is not dependent. Therefore, nothing could be in relationship. Since everything exists in dependence, reification thereby rejects everything. By rejecting everything, those who reify reality have rejected all causes.

The seventeenth verse continues the argument. By rejecting all causes, those who think that to exist is to be nonempty and to be empty is to be nonexistent must also reject results dependent on these causes. If they reject all results that depend on their causes, this means that language and our thinking must also be rejected. This means the agent, his actions, and the objects of those actions would all be categorically rejected by the opponent. Furthermore, since cause and effects are rejected, this means the opponent must reject the very production and disintegration of things. Thus, those who reify reality actually reject everything. They reject all things and all events.

The heart of the chapter—and of the book—is presented in the eighteenth verse. Understanding this verse properly becomes the cornerstone of correctly understanding the Middle Way. Whatever dependently originates is empty of existing intrinsically. There are only two possibilities: either things exist objectively from their own side, or they exist subjectively from the side of the mind. Existing from the side of the mind means they are dependently designated by the mind. Rejecting things existing intrinsically from the side of the object means they must exist subjectively through dependent designation. This is the identity of emptiness and dependent arising. *Emptiness* means absence of intrinsic or independent existence. Absence of intrinsic or independent existence means dependent origination. What is dependently arisen is explained as emptiness. Even this identity itself is a dependent designation. This is the Middle Way. This is the powerful meaning of verse 18:

18. Whatever is dependently originated
is explained to be emptiness.
That, being a dependent designation,
is itself the Middle Way.

Not only is the identity of dependent arising and emptiness a dependent designation, but *everything* is a dependent designation, being dependently arisen. As everything is dependently arisen, everything is empty. This includes all phenomena, as stated in verse 19:

19. There does not exist anything
that is not dependently originated.
Therefore, there does not exist
anything that is not empty.

Thus, these two verses in chapter 24, verse 18 and verse 19, distill the essence of Nāgārjuna's *Fundamental Verses on the Middle Way*. The Dalai Lama says he recites, reflects upon, and meditates on these two verses daily, and he advises us to do the same. This is a pith instruction from a realized master: Nothing exists that is not dependent on others. Therefore, nothing exists intrinsically. The Dalai Lama often teaches that this verse is the essence of the whole text. Thus, these verses summarize Nāgārjuna's important work. They are also an important instruction to deepen our understanding.

The twentieth verse goes on: If all phenomena were not empty of intrinsic existence, then there would be no production and no disintegration. If there were no production and no disintegration, then the four noble truths would be impossible.

The twenty-first verse argues, if things did not depend on others, then how could suffering be produced? The Buddha taught that phenomena are impermanent and that all contaminated things are in the nature of suffering. This precludes the possibility that things could exist from their own side intrinsically.

Moreover, if things did in fact exist intrinsically, how could they ever be produced? Those who reify reality would be rejecting everything in the world, all things and events, since all are produced. As those who reify reality would reject all phenomena, including production, they would therefore also reject the cause of suffering. This is the conclusion drawn in the twenty-second verse.

Furthermore, if suffering existed intrinsically, then the cessation of suffering would be impossible. As the cessation of suffering would be impossible, suffering would last forever. In this way, those who reify reality are forced into a position whereby they must reject the cessation of suffering based on their own logic. This is the presentation in the twenty-third verse.

If the path existed intrinsically, then how could there be meditation? When those who reify reality propose a path to enlightenment that complements meditation, that path cannot exist intrinsically. For if it did exist intrinsically, the absurd consequence would follow that we could never relate to that path. Without relating to the path, we could never meditate on the path. This is the further absurd consequence of intrinsic existence drawn out in the twenty-fourth verse.

Following from the logic of those who reify reality, there would be no suffering, no cause of suffering, and no cessation of suffering. If that were the case, the twenty-fifth verse questions, then precisely who is it that attains the cessation of suffering?

And if there is no one who attains the cessation of suffering, then no truth could be realized at the ultimate level. Hence, there would be no ultimate truth of reality to be realized. Therefore, the twenty-sixth verse concludes, the truth concerning reality, which is the object of meditation, cannot possibly exist intrinsically.

Furthermore, if all these things existed intrinsically, then it would be impossible for those who reify reality to continue maintaining their position of knowing, abandoning, cultivating, and actualizing all the achievements that result from meditation on the truth of reality. The twenty-seventh verse again demonstrates the absurdity of objective, intrinsic existence by showing how it contradicts complete understanding, abandonment, cultivation, and actualization.

These important products of meditation on emptiness could never come about since intrinsically existent achievement could never be. How could there be any achievement at all in the face of an unchanging, inert world that is devoid of relations? This is the conclusion drawn in the twenty-eighth verse.

Without attainment, there could be no arhats reaching and abiding in these attainments. Without those stream-entering arhats putting effort into attainments, the eight kinds of arhats could not exist. The twenty-ninth verse concludes that without these eight kinds of arhats there would be no Saṅgha. If there were no four noble truths, which are the truths from the perspective of these arhats, then there would be no Dharma. And if there were no Dharma and no Saṅgha, then how could there be a Buddha?

Nāgārjuna skillfully turns all the arguments addressed to the Prāsaṅgikas back onto their originators and rightful owners, those who reify reality. He states that these faults do not attach to the Prāsaṅgika position; rather, they attach to any position that reifies reality. This is the grand finale; this is the presentation of the thirtieth verse.

According to those who reify reality, a buddha would not be dependent on enlightenment, nor would enlightenment be dependent on a buddha. This further absurd consequence of grasping intrinsic existence, which prevents any type of relationship at all, is presented in the thirty-first verse by the Prāsaṅgikas.

Furthermore, according to those who reify reality, those who have not yet attained enlightenment could never practice the path to enlightenment. Intrinsic existence does not allow anything to change. Thus, there could be no transformation; hence, no one could ever practice the path. This is a further absurd consequence of intrinsic existence presented by Nāgārjuna in the thirty-second verse.

If the view of intrinsic existence of those who reify reality is to be accepted, this means that no one could ever know the difference between Dharma and non-Dharma. In this context, *Dharma* and *non-Dharma* refer to virtue and nonvirtue; thus, no one could ever distinguish between right and wrong. If things were not empty of intrinsic existence, nothing at all would ever be possible. The impossibility of anything, anywhere at any time, is a further absurd consequence of the view of intrinsic existence of those who reify reality, laid out in the thirty-third verse.

Furthermore, as made clear in the thirty-fourth verse, if there is no practice of morality and immorality, then according to those who think that to exist is to be nonempty and to be empty is to be nonexistent, nobody could ever attain any results. Intrinsic existence prevents all relationships, including causality. Without causes there can be no results.

Yet those who reify reality continue insisting that results are produced from moral and immoral actions. In that case, then why are morality and immorality not empty of intrinsic existence? If results are produced from moral and immoral actions, then these actions must be empty of intrinsic existence. Intrinsic existence precludes any change, any causality. This is a further contradiction of intrinsic existence. Verse 35 exposes the absurdity that no results could ever be produced.

The thirty-sixth verse concludes that in actuality those who reify reality are rejecting all conventional phenomena whatsoever at any time and at any place. Thus, they are completely rejecting dependent origination.

Therefore, for those who reify reality there would be no striving to attain anything. They are forced into the ridiculous position that performance of action would be devoid of any activity and any object. Action without activity and action without an object are the further absurd consequences explained in the thirty-seventh verse.

If that were the case, then nobody would do anything. Without activity and without an object, it would be impossible to do anything. If beings existed intrinsically, then they could not be born, and if beings are not born, neither could they die—leading to the absurd result of unborn beings who can never die. All change and transformation is precluded. Thus, they would be completely bereft of any attributes or any relationships at all. Complete inert inactivity is the absurd consequence of intrinsic existence drawn out in the thirty-eighth verse.

When those who reify reality reject emptiness, this implies that beings possessing lesser results could not attain higher results. Hence, no one would be freed from karma and delusions and no one could attain freedom from suffering. The thirty-ninth verse shows the absurd consequence that the third and fourth noble truths would be utterly impossible given the view of reification. Thus, whoever correctly sees the true meaning of dependent origination will understand conditioned pervasive suffering. They will then recognize the cause of suffering and hence will attain cessation from that suffering. Nāgārjuna shows here in the fortieth and last verse that understanding emptiness is equivalent to understanding the four noble truths, precisely what the opponent claimed could not be understood within the framework of emptiness. The four noble truths are a metaphor for understanding everything one needs to understand. And they are exactly what the opponent claimed that Nāgārjuna himself undermined.

Nāgārjuna thus demonstrates that the opponent's view of reification leads him to fall into nihilism. Contrary to the opponent's opinion, the view of emptiness enables affirmation of conventional reality of the phenomenon in question. This chapter therefore shows that it is only the Madhyamaka position that allows one to affirm the Buddhadharma. Reification looks like it it is called in to save the Dharma from Madhyamaka nihilism, but in fact just the opposite occurs. Reification actually becomes the nihilism.

This important chapter follows previous exhaustive refutations of intrinsic existence, which might have left some wondering if all existence has been totally rejected. Thus, chapter 24 establishes conventional reality of the important ground, path, and result. The thorough establishment of conventional reality within the context of emptiness is the grand achievement of Nāgārjuna, clearly elucidating the thought of the Buddha.

# 4. The Tathāgata

of Nāgārjuna's *Fundamental Verses
on the Middle Way*

Because chapter 24 establishes conventional reality through the understanding of emptiness, some might think there is something quite special about emptiness. And of course there is. But some might also draw the conclusion there is something absolute about it. To counter such a misinterpretation, Nāgārjuna presents chapter 22, "Analysis of the Tathāgata." Even the Buddha is empty of intrinsic existence—and by implication, so is the ultimate nature of the Buddha. Thus, emptiness itself is empty. This chapter is important because there is a tendency to reify things that are taken to be sacred, that are given some kind of special existential status.

The Buddha, in order to benefit sentient beings, accumulated vast amounts of merit and understanding and wisdom over countless lifetimes. Through these efforts he attained buddhahood. Since the attainment of buddhahood requires innumerable lifetimes of enormous effort practicing the path, some say this continuum of lifetimes must exist intrinsically. For without them, how could someone attain buddhahood? Therefore, since his continuum of lifetimes exists intrinsically, so must the Buddha exist intrinsically. Nāgārjuna will argue in chapter 22 that ultimately there can be no such thing as a Buddha.

### Root Verses of Chapter 22

1. Buddha is neither one with nor distinct from
   the aggregates.
The aggregates are not in him, nor is he in them.
The Buddha does not possess the aggregates.
Then how could there be a Buddha?

2. If the Buddha who is dependent on the
   aggregates
does not exist intrinsically,
how could something that does not exist
   intrinsically
exist [by depending] intrinsically on others?

3. Whatever depends on another
cannot exist intrinsically on its own.
That which does not exist intrinsically on its own—
how could it be a Buddha?

4. If there is no intrinsic self-nature,
how could there be an intrinsic other?
Apart from an intrinsic self and other,
how could there be a Buddha?

5. Without depending on the aggregates,
if [earlier] there were a Tathāgata,
now he would depend upon them.
Depending on them, he becomes [the
    appropriator].

6. There is no Buddha whatsoever
not depending on his aggregates.
If [earlier] he did not exist without depending [on
    them],
how could he become the appropriator?

7. Without the appropriated
there is no appropriation.
Without appropriation
how could there be a Buddha?

8. Having searched in the fivefold way,
how can the Tathāgata who is neither one nor
distinct be posited as [existing intrinsically]
by its appropriation?

9. Whatever is appropriated
cannot exist intrinsically.
By not existing through its own nature,
it cannot exist through the nature of another.

10. Thus appropriated and appropriator
are empty in every respect.
How could an empty Buddha be
established by empty designation?

11. We do not assert "empty."
We do not assert "nonempty."
We assert neither both nor neither.
They are asserted for the sake of designation.

12. The four [tetralemma] such as permanence,
impermanence, etc.—
how could these exist in the one who is free?
The four [tetralemma] such as with and without
an end—
how could these exist in the one who is free?

13. [According to the Tibetan translation of
Buddhapālita,] the one who strongly grasps
[at the true existence of things]
will conceptualize in his mind

the existence or nonexistence of
the Tathāgata in nirvana.

14. Being empty of intrinsic nature,
the thought of the Buddha either
[intrinsically] existing or not existing
after attaining nirvāṇa is senseless.

15. Those who fabricate the Buddha,
who is beyond [all] fabrications and ceaseless,
all of them who are damaged by fabrication,
will not see the Buddha.

16. Whatever is the nature of the Tathāgata
is also the nature of transmigrators.
The Tathāgata has no intrinsic nature;
[likewise] the transmigrators have no intrinsic
   nature.

In chapter 24, Nāgārjuna related the subtleties of the four
noble truths, particularly cessation (emptiness), to their
characteristics, or nature; function; and result, or outcome of practice, to the essential framework of Buddhist
practice; he related the subtle aspects of the four noble
truths to the essential framework of the ground, path, and
result, or outcome of practice. In doing so, some might

interpret Nāgārjuna as glorifying emptiness into something absolute. To counter any such ideas, Nāgārjuna presents chapter 22, "Analysis of the Tathāgata."

In chapter 22, Nāgārjuna argues that even emptiness itself is empty of any intrinsic existence. As we saw in verses 18 and 19 of chapter 24, "Analysis of the Four Noble Truths," *emptiness* has the same meaning as dependent origination, so it cannot be independent or intrinsic.

The first verse in chapter 22 states that the Buddha cannot exist intrinsically. For if he did exist intrinsically, then when analyzing an intrinsically existent Buddha, such a Buddha would have to be found. Yet this is not the case. He is neither one with his uncontaminated aggregates, nor is he distinct from his uncontaminated aggregates. Nor does he (intrinsically) exist in his uncontaminated aggregates. Nor do the uncontaminated aggregates (intrinsically) exist in the Buddha. *Existing in* means neither is the Buddha an intrinsic base for his aggregates nor is the uncontaminated aggregates an intrinsic base for the Buddha. Thus, the Buddha does not intrinsically depend on his aggregates, nor do the aggregates intrinsically depend on the Buddha.

These four points establish the absence of an intrinsic Buddha and intrinsic aggregates. This suggests they can only exist through mutual dependence. This is exactly the same argument rejecting the intrinsic existence of any being and of all phenomena, not just the Tathāgata.

Finally, the Buddha does not intrinsically possess his uncontaminated aggregates. This is the last point of Nāgārjuna's fivefold analysis investigating the deeper existence of a Buddha. In the end such a Buddha cannot be intrinsically found.

The analysis of fivefold extremes is sometimes referred to as the *analysis of the five corners*. There are no other possibilities. The argument boils down to two alternatives, as we have said before. For something to exist, it must be either the same as its basis of designation, here the aggregates (for a person), or different. Thus, the fivefold analysis is an elaboration on these two possibilities, *same* or *different*, and is a slightly abbreviated version of the seven-fold analysis.

Next, Nāgārjuna searches for the Buddha among the collection of his uncontaminated aggregates and among the shape of his uncontaminated aggregates; this becomes the sevenfold analysis searching for the ultimate truth, or existential status, of the Buddha.

The sevenfold analysis is a further expansion of the fivefold analysis and is presented by Candrakīrti in *Entering the Middle Way* in his analogy of a chariot. This sevenfold analysis is presented using a chariot as an example but is applicable to the analysis of the self and all phenomena as well. If the chariot were to exist intrinsically, then during the careful investigation for the chariot, its essential chariot nature must be found either within the chariot as a whole or within its parts.

What is it that we are analyzing? The object of negation must be recognized correctly. When we see the chariot without analyzing its existence, we think, "This is a chariot." The referent object of the term *chariot* appears as if it invisibly covers or envelops the collection of parts like a transparent blanket. We have preconceptions about an independent, partless, enduring chariot even before we lay eyes on it.

The crux of the sevenfold analysis is sameness or difference. The chariot is not intrinsically identical with the parts. If the parts were the chariot, there would be many contradictions. Since the parts are many, there would be many chariots. Or as the chariot is one, so all the parts would have to be one; the agent (chariot) and the parts (object) would be the same.

Nor is the chariot and its parts intrinsically separate; if they were, like a flower and a glass of milk, then the chariot would be seen as separate from the parts. But it is not. Furthermore, the chariot and the parts would be unrelated.

The chariot is also not the basis for the parts, like a water tank holding water. Nor does the chariot rest in the parts, like Reinhold Messner precariously perched on the side of a mountain in his bivouac sack. This would be true only if the chariot and the parts were intrinsically separate (completely unrelated), which they are not. They are definitely related.

The chariot possessing the parts is also untenable. If this possession is like a nerd possessing a MacBook Pro—that is, an object other than himself—then the chariot and the parts should be seen separately. But they are not. If, on the other hand, possession is like the nerd possessing his nerdy brain, we are now refuting intrinsic oneness, and intrinsic oneness or sameness has already been refuted.

Candrakīrti explains in *Entering the Middle Way*, chapter 6:

> A chariot is not asserted to be different from
>     its parts,
> nor is it non-different, nor does it possess them;
> it is not in the parts, nor is it the owner of the parts.
> It is not the mere collection of them nor is it
>     their shape.[24]

The chariot is not the collection of parts; if it were, then those parts lying around in a disorderly fashion would be the chariot. The collection of parts is not the chariot, so too the shape of this collection of parts is not the chariot. Also, is the chariot the shape of the collection of parts or of the individual parts? If the chariot is the shape of the individual parts, then is the shape of the parts the same before and after the parts are assembled?

Or is the shape of the parts after assembly different from the shape of the parts prior to the assembly?

Candrakīrti further explains in *Entering the Middle Way*:

> If the mere collection of parts were a chariot,
> Then a chariot would exist even while its parts lie
>     in pieces.
> Without the whole, the parts do not exist.
> Hence the mere shape also cannot be the chariot.

> If you say the shape that each part already had
> Is what we know as the chariot,
> Then just as there is no chariot when the parts
>     are unassembled,
> So it is also [there is no shape] when they are
>     assembled.

> If now while the chariot is here,
> There were a different shape in the wheels
>     and such,
> Then it would be evident, but it is not.
> Therefore, the mere shape is not a chariot.

> According to you, collections do not exist at all,
> So the shape cannot be that of the collection
>     of parts.

How could you see a chariot in the shape
Of something that does not exist at all?[25]

Finally, Candrakīrti tells us that when we have determined that every one of the seven possibilities is refuted for one thing, we should repeat this analysis until we develop certainty there is no intrinsic existence anywhere, any time, in any thing:

As this is what you assert,
You should also understand that all effects
That have untrue natures are produced
In dependence upon untrue causes.[26]

Subsequently, when we see the chariot, we cannot deny the appearance, even though there is no intrinsic existence. Tsongkhapa writes in the special insight section of *The Great Treatise on the Stages to the Path of Enlightenment*:

Oh, it is amazing how the magicians of karma
and the afflictions conjure up these illusions, such
as chariots![27]

And he continues:

You will be certain that dependent arising means
that things are not intrinsically produced. As

Candrakīrti's *Commentary on the Four Hundred
Verses on the Yogic Deeds of Bodhisattvas* (*Bodhisattva-
yogācāracatuḥśatakaṭīkā*) says:

> Pots and such do not exist under the fivefold
> analysis as to whether they are the same as their
> causes or other than their causes. Nevertheless,
> through dependent imputation, they can do
> things like hold or scoop honey, or water, or
> milk. Is this not wonderful?[28]

Tsongkhapa counsels us that just understanding things
as merely projected is not enough. This, he says, is relatively easy. The more subtle and difficult part to understand is that it *still functions.* As Candrakīrti says, "Is this
not wonderful?"

This wonderment at the functionality of conventional
existence embedded within emptiness is expressed in verse
88 of *A Commentary on the Awakening Mind* (*Bodhicitta-
vivaraṇa*) by Nāgārjuna:

> Those who understand this emptiness of phenomena
> Yet also conform to the law of karma and its results,
> That is more amazing than amazing!
> That is more wondrous than wondrous![29]

In the second verse of *Fundamental Verses on the Middle Way*, Nāgārjuna further points out that because he is dependently imputed upon his aggregates, the Buddha cannot exist intrinsically. Because of this his aggregates would also not exist intrinsically. Because he is dependently imputed, he exists like a reflection in a mirror. That which has no intrinsic nature of its own—how could it exist intrinsically by depending on others?

Yet if the Buddha did exist intrinsically, then he would have to exist without depending on his aggregates. This is the dilemma facing the defenders of intrinsic existence as presented in the third verse. Since an intrinsically real Buddha does not exist separate from or identical to his aggregates, the Buddha cannot exist intrinsically at all. This verse emphasizes the fact that these two possibilities of being *one* with the bases of designation and *distinct* from these bases are complete. They are mutually exclusive. There is no third possibility. This is the conclusion presented in the fourth verse.

The fifth verse challenges the position of the Saṃmitīya school. That school is one of eighteen schools of Vaibhashika that assert that the Buddha is neither one with nor distinct from his aggregates. They argue a third possibility beyond sameness and difference defying the logic of the excluded middle. They argue that the Buddha is inexpressible but intrinsically existent. If there did exist a Buddha without depending on his aggregates, as they assert, then he would have to depend on his aggregates and possess them. However, an intrinsic Buddha independent of his aggregates is untenable with reality. The opponent who thinks that a Buddha is independent of his aggregates cannot make sense of the Buddha being in relation to the aggregates. But he must be in relationship with his aggregates if we are to explain a Buddha's attainments and activities. This is the meaning of the fifth verse.

The sixth verse offers the reason. If the Buddha never depended on his aggregates, then he could never possess the aggregates. Without his aggregates the Buddha would never be perceived. Nor could he ever function. Moreover, if he never depended on the aggregates, how could he ever claim the aggregates as his own?

If the Buddha never adopts the aggregates, then his aggregates could never be appropriated. In that case he would be without any aggregates. Without the appropriated aggregates there could never be an appropriator. Thus, those who reify reality are forced into the conclusion that there cannot be a Buddha. Then if there were no Buddha, who would appropriate the uncontaminated aggregates? This argument, starting with no appropriated aggregates and leading to the conclusion that therefore there would be no appropriator, the Buddha, is the presentation found in the seventh verse.

The eighth verse concludes, having investigated in these five comprehensive ways, that no Buddha can be identified as identical or separate from the aggregates. Thus, the Buddha cannot be the intrinsic appropriator of his aggregates.

In a similar way, the aggregates to be appropriated also do not intrinsically exist. As the appropriator or the self does not exist separately from the aggregates, then how could the aggregates to be appropriated exist separately from the self? Restating this argument, we could say that when the self does not exist separately from the aggregates, then the aggregates do not exist separately from the self. This ninth verse follows closely on the heels of the eighth verse.

From all these arguments, verse 10 concludes that both the appropriator and the appropriated are empty of intrinsic existence. Thus, the Buddha is empty of intrinsic existence. Therefore, it is contradictory to continue maintaining that the Buddha intrinsically exists. This is the conclusion drawn from the tenth verse.

The emptiness of the Buddha is established in the eleventh verse. The analysis of the Buddha is no different from the analysis of any other phenomena, and emptiness in the context of the Buddha has no separate, higher meaning. Emptiness is the same regardless of the base that is empty.

The logical strategy adopted here utilizes the argument of the tetralemma. Also called "reasoning utilizing the four extremes or four corners," the structure of the tetralemma is that, regarding any logical argument, there are four and only four possibilities: affirmation, negation, both affirmation and negation, and neither. The Buddha, like all phenomena, is not empty because it exists. The Buddha, like all phenomena, is not nonempty because it is empty of intrinsic existence. Furthermore, the Buddha is neither both, nor neither. This is because phenomena exist by designation. This has everything to do with the understanding of what speech does, and with the relationship between conventional and ultimate. This verse is tied to the parallel verse 10 in chapter 24:

> Without a basis of conventional truth,
> the ultimate truth cannot be taught.
> Without understanding the ultimate,
> nirvāṇa cannot be attained.

This verse is about where you go when you are done depending on the conventional. It is also about the point of depending on the conventional. When we are establishing reality, we must take care not to fall into either extreme of nihilism or reification. Conventionally, saying things are not empty means we avoid the extreme of nihilism where nothing exists. By establishing their ultimate nature, the absence of intrinsic existence, we avoid the extreme of reification. Once we have established that things are not nonexistent and do not exist from their own side, what reality is there? If things exist and do not exist from their own side objectively, then they must be established subjectively. Therefore, things must be established solely based upon mental designation.

The twelfth verse further generalizes the argument to all composed phenomena. All composed phenomena are neither intrinsically permanent, nor intrinsically impermanent, nor both, nor neither. This succinct and powerful tetralemma reasoning negates all fabrications of intrinsic existence. Thus, there are no phenomena existing intrinsically at any time or anywhere. Moreover, the world is neither intrinsically finite, nor intrinsically infinite, nor both, nor neither. When things are established subjectively through designation, the role of speech and thought becomes paramount in establishing reality.

Those who reify reality and continue to view the Buddha as existing intrinsically are clouded by the fog of dense ignorance. They confuse *nonintrinsic existence* to mean no existence at all. This is the word of caution expressed in the thirteenth verse.

*Fundamental Verses on the Middle Way* was initially translated into Tibetan by Chogro Luyi Gyaltsen. Later it was edited by the Tibetan translator Patsap Nyima Drakpa. There are two versions in Tibetan of chapter

22, verse 13. One is consistent with the Tibetan translation of *Buddhapālita*, and the other is consistent with the Tibetan translation of Candrakīrti's *Clear Words*. We have chosen to use the translation that is consistent with *Buddhapālita*; Tsongkhapa in his *Ocean of Reasoning* states it is the better one. In the translation that is consistent with *Clear Words*, the last lines have only "nonexistence" and do not include "existence." Regarding the *Fundamental Verses on the Middle Way* in Sanskrit: scholars write this thirteenth verse is ambiguous.

From the perspective of the understanding of the emptiness of intrinsic existence, no doubts whatsoever will ever arise concerning the existence of the Buddha and the existence of nirvāṇa. Thus, with respect to this correct view, as stated in the fourteenth verse, there is no danger of falling into either extreme of permanence or nihilism. Therefore, everything is established seamlessly, and everything makes perfect sense.

> These twelve views and the two views that one's life is either identical to or different from one's body are said to be the fourteen views to which the Buddha would not assent. This is because since all of these presuppose the inherent existence of the self, these questions received no answer. Those who asked these questions were not vessels of the profound; therefore, it was inappropriate to explain the mean-

ing of selflessness to them. Even had he explained such things as permanence and impermanence, that would have given rise to either reification or nihilism and so would have served no purpose.[30]

Those clouded by fabrications of self-grasping cannot see the Buddha because their ignorance precludes the possibility of attaining Buddhahood. Everyone who thinks that to exist is to be nonempty and to be empty is to be nonexistent is obscured from seeing the possibility of attaining buddhahood. This possibility of attaining Buddhahood is recognized once ignorance is understood as distorted reality. This is because this is the state in which all fabrications cease. The fifteenth verse explains this fundamental obscuration hindering freedom and liberation from all suffering.

All sentient beings have the same nature as the Buddha. As the Buddha lacks intrinsic nature, likewise sentient beings also lack intrinsic nature. This means the ultimate nature of nirvāṇa and saṃsāra is the same. This is the profound conclusion drawn in the sixteenth and last verse of chapter 22, "Analysis of the Tathāgata."

# 5. Conditions

## CHAPTER 1
## of Nāgārjuna's *Fundamental Verses on the Middle Way*

In *Fundamental Verses on the Middle Way,* Nāgārjuna expounds the same view as the prajñāpāramitā sūtras: that all things are dependently produced, free from the eight extremes. The principal topic of the prajñāpāramitā sūtras is emptiness. In order to do away with self-grasping and the misery that follows it, Nāgārjuna taught the profound view of emptiness. He also taught the dependent nature of all things. These two, emptiness and dependent arising, are analogous to two sides of the same coin.

This chapter, "Analysis of Conditions," focuses on *pratītyasamutpāda,* or production in dependence on causes and conditions. This is the more general first level of the three levels of dependent origination we discussed in the introduction: dependence on production through causes and conditions, dependence of the whole on its parts and of the parts on the whole, and dependence on designation.

This first chapter of *Fundamental Verses on the Middle Way*, "Analysis of Conditions," has three sections. The first section, the salutation and verse 1, refutes intrinsic production. The second section, verses 2–10, refutes the four conditions mentioned in verse 2 individually. The third section, verses 11–14, is the conclusion and refutes an intrinsic effect.

### Root Verses of Chapter 1

I prostrate to the perfect Buddha,
the best of all teachers,
who taught that dependent origination is
free of cessation, and free of production,
without disintegration, and without permanence,
without coming, and without going,
without distinction or oneness,
and peaceful in total extinction
of all conceptual fabrications.

1. Neither from itself nor from another,
nor from both nor without a cause
is anything, anywhere, at any time,
ever produced.

2. There are four conditions:
the causal, the objective,
the proximate, and the dominant.
There is no fifth condition.

3. An intrinsic nature of things
does not exist in its conditions, etc.
If the entity that is self does not exist,
the entity that is other does not exist.

4. An action does not have conditions;
no action exists without conditions.
Although there are no conditions without an
    action,
[conditions] do have an action still.

5. They are *called* conditions by virtue
of something arising in dependence on them.
When nothing arises [in dependence] on them,
how can they not be called nonconditions?

6. Even in regard to nonexistent or existent objects
the condition is untenable.
Because if nonexistent, what would it be the
    condition of?
If existent, what is the need for a condition?

7.  When a phenomenon is neither established
as existent, nonexistent, nor both,
how could that which establishes be called a cause?
If that is the case, [a causal condition] is
    unfeasible.

8.  [You] have emphatically stated an existent
    entity
[mind] has no object.
If this entity [mind] has no object,
how can an object of perception be possible?

9.  If phenomena do not arise,
cessation becomes unfeasible.
Therefore, a proximate [condition] is untenable.
If things have ceased, what then is a condition?

10.  Since there is no existence in things
lacking intrinsic nature,
the statement "because this exists, that arises"
is not acceptable.

11.  The effect is not in the conditions
individually or collectively.
Thus how could something not in
the conditions be produced from them?

12. However, despite the result being nonexistent
[in the conditions]
if it arises from these conditions,
why would it not arise
from nonconditions?

13. If the effect had the nature of the conditions,
conditions would not have their own nature.
How can an effect (which arises) from that which
lacks
its own self-entity be in the nature of conditions?

14. Therefore, there is no result that is of
the nature of the conditions or nonconditions.
And since the result is nonexistent,
how can something be [its] condition or
noncondition?

## The First Section:
## Refutation of the Eight Extremes

In the salutation that begins this chapter, Nāgārjuna pays homage to the fully enlightened one, who is supreme among all teachers. Of all the great teachers who have appeared in this world as founders of various traditions and religions, Nāgārjuna regards the Buddha as the supreme. Therefore, from the depths of his heart Nāgārjuna pays homage to the Buddha.

The Buddha is the supreme of all teachers because he was the first to teach the profound doctrine of emptiness. Others within the Buddhist tradition, like Nāgārjuna, have taught this profound emptiness, but none outside this tradition have been able to do so. Tsongkhapa also praises Śākyamuni Buddha for these same qualities of wisdom in verse 7 of his *In Praise of Dependent Origination* (*Rten 'brel bstod pa*):

> Since this teaching is not seen elsewhere,
> You alone are the Teacher;
> Like calling fox a lion, for a Tirthika
> It would be a word of flattery.

And continues in verse 37:

> Among teachers, the teacher of dependent origination,
> Amongst wisdoms, the knowledge of dependent
>    origination—
> You, who're most excellent like the kings in the worlds,
> Know this perfectly well, not others.[31]

Toward the end of the salutation (the last two lines in English and the third-to-last line in Tibetan), we see these lines:

**Peaceful in total extinction
of all conceptual fabrications.**

In Tibetan, this is *spros pa nyer zhi zhi bstan pa*.[32]
*Spros pa* means "fabrication." One kind of fabrication is
reification, and that is the subject of the homage verses,
though it can also mean "elaboration." The reification
in this instance comprises the eight extremes of intrinsic production, intrinsic cessation, and so forth. Thus,
reification exaggerates more existence in things than is
actually there. It qualifies things and events as intrinsic,
objective, and independent. In reality things are not intrinsically produced, they do not intrinsically cease, and
so on. Rather, things and events exist merely through
designation. Designation takes place through the designating mind and is expressed by words. The basis of designation is that which is taken into consideration when
addressing or referring to something, such as a person. It
is usually expressed in words and concepts. The various
parts of the body, as well as the mind and speech of the
person, are used to speak of the person. Without them
we cannot properly speak of the person. The basis of designation is always something that is not the person when
speaking of the person. If all parts, or the whole, or even
something distinct from the aggregates are said to be the
person, then multiple contradictions would follow. The
same would follow for all other phenomena. The basis for

the designation comprises the parts of a thing. The process of designation includes the basis of designation, the context, and the designating mind. Failure to see this, and the tendency to ascribe the thing intrinsic identity, is reification, *spros pa*.

*Zhi ba* means "peaceful." The eight links that conventionally exist do not appear to the nonconceptual mind, which is absorbed in emptiness. Thus emptiness, referred to as *dependent origination* here, that appears to the yogic mind, which nonconceptually perceives the ultimate reality, is free from elaboration. This is what *pacified* means. If the eight links existed intrinsically, they would be ultimate reality. In that case, they would have to appear to the nonconceptual mind of an ārya being, which perceives the ultimate reality. But they do not. Such a mind does not conceptualize either in primary minds or mental factors. Being free of the perceiver and the perception conventionally, the mind that dwells nonconceptually in emptiness has no birth, aging, sickness, or any other miseries. Therefore, such a mind is free, and this is what *freedom* in this context means.

The main theme of Nāgārjuna's text is dependent origination free from the eight extremes of intrinsic reality, which has the same meaning as emptiness free from these eight extremes. This is explained using numerous arguments and scriptural citations. Nāgārjuna is not arguing that these different characteristics of things—ceasing, production, disintegrating, permanent, coming, going, distinct, one—do not exist at all. Of course they exist. But they exist *conventionally*. Nāgārjuna argues that they do not exist *intrinsically*.

The main argument Nāgārjuna uses to prove that things do not have intrinsic production, cessation, and so forth, relies on the notion of dependent origination. Each of these eight characteristics arises in dependence on many causes and conditions.

If something has intrinsic cessation, it would either continually be in the process of ceasing or never cease. On the other hand, with dependently originated cessation, everything exists in dependence on other factors, so when the cause for something's existence is exhausted, that thing would cease to exist.

Intrinsic oneness means something would either always be one or would never be one. But dependently originated oneness depends upon difference, for without difference there could not be oneness. Things would exist in relationship. This is not possible with intrinsic existence.

Usually, when we refer to something as *permanent* or *impermanent*, it is on the basis of whether it continues to undergo change or not over time. If something is intrinsically permanent or intrinsically impermanent, there is no dependence on time. Without depending on time, we cannot talk about a continuum's continuation or exhaustion.

Intrinsic coming and going would not allow any motion, for motion requires relationship, moving from *here* to *there*, and particularly cause and effect. And intrinsic existence precludes any relationship whatsoever. Dependently originated coming and going would allow for motion due to relationship such as causality. Thus the lifting of a foot, for example, gives rise to either coming or going.

Therefore, dependent origination explains why things are produced and cease, are one or distinct, are enduring or fleeting, and in motion—in each case, conventionally. If things existed intrinsically, they could not be produced, cease, retain identity, be different from anything else, endure, disintegrate, or be in motion.

This first chapter of *Fundamental Verses on the Middle Way* is devoted to explaining that things have no intrinsic production, and why.

When we say something *is produced*, this means there is a cause for that production; without a cause for production there can be no production. Furthermore, without the *action of producing*, which means the meeting of the cause with its effect, there can be no production. Take, for example, a sprout. The substantial cause for a sprout is its seed. So when the seed is about to germinate, and the sprout is about to arise, the meeting of these two is involved in the action of producing the sprout. We could simply say this is the meeting of the cause and the effect. The seed needs to give rise to the sprout. Nāgārjuna will refute that this meeting of cause and effect is an intrinsic meeting.

On a subtler level, production comes about by mental designation—through the assemblage of words, language, and concepts. What we take to be the cause of something, or the effect, has to do with our explanatory interests. From one perspective, the seed is the cause. From another, a seed is the result of its own cause and therefore is the result. However, intrinsically it is neither a cause nor a result. Only in dependence upon its cause is it a result. And only in dependence upon its result is it a cause. Thus intrinsicality is totally mistaken.

Thus, when we say something is produced, the statement is posited on the basis of multiple factors coming together. Without this assemblage of multiple factors, there can be no production, and there is no separate thing that is independent of these factors. This is the reality of phenomena.

But this is not how things appear to us. Ordinarily, when we see things, we perceive them as standing over "there," as solid and independent. They seem to be existing from their own side in and of themselves rather than depending on other factors like their production, our mind, and so on. Due to these appearances we cling to solid and independently produced things. If things were produced independently or intrinsically, this would be contradictory. Production and intrinsic production are opposites, like light and darkness. To be produced refutes being independent; to exist intrinsically refutes being dependent.

Those who reify reality do so in large part because they are committed to intrinsic production. They maintain that things are produced from their causes. For those who reify reality, effects are produced from causes intrinsically. For them, if intrinsic causes and effects did not establish intrinsic production, then nothing could exist at all. Without intrinsic production there could be no production. Thus, they conclude things possess intrinsic nature. Due to this fundamental misunderstanding of dependent origination, those who reify reality grasp at intrinsic production. Production is how all conditioned things come into existence. Thus, to counter this crucial mistake that underlies many other wrong views, Nāgārjuna begins *Fundamental Verses on the Middle Way* by refuting intrinsic production from causes. The fundamental wisdom that refutes intrinsic production is the starting point for Nāgārjuna's critique of wrong views.

Nāgārjuna uses tetralemma reasoning to establish the lack of intrinsic production; he argues that if there were intrinsic production, then effects would necessarily be caused through one of four alternatives: (1) Things arising from themselves intrinsically would continually arise, never arise, would be senseless to arise again, and the three—agent, action, and object—would become one. (2) Things arising from others would be different. If they were intrinsically different, they could never interact, as there would never be contact. Hence, things could not transform from one thing into another. Things would never change. Everything could arise from everything else. For example, a flame can give rise to darkness. (3) Things arising intrinsically both from self and other: each of these possibilities has been already refuted. (4) Things arising without a cause: if they could, then anything could produce anything. In that case, effort to become a better human being would be wasted. Planting seeds would not yield crops so would be a waste of energy and resources. Without a cause, a result is impossible.

Explicitly using the tetralemma argumentation, Nāgārjuna concludes there is no intrinsic production.

The first verse in Nāgārjuna's *Fundamental Verses on the Middle Way* states there is no production from any of the four alternatives with respect to intrinsic nature; things are not produced from themselves, or from another, or from both, or from neither. There are different views from various scholars as to whether Nāgārjuna is using *reductio ad absurdum*—a method of argumentation that takes an opponent's theory to its logical conclusion in order to demonstrate its absurdity—or positive arguments.

Generally speaking, in order to show some contradiction within the system of the opponent, the reductio arguments are used. Examine, for example, the opponent's argument for production that takes intrinsic existence for granted; Nāgārjuna argues that intrinsic production cannot produce anything. The reductio exposes contradictions in the opponent's reasoning, thereby shaking his previously held truths. In this way he comes to doubt his own thesis.

A reductio ad absurdum argument does not, however, demonstrate the truth of an alternative position. A positive argument (syllogistic) does; it is an argument for a conclusion to be accepted by the opponent that offers premises and reasoning to support it; for example, sound is impermanent because it is produced, and all produced things are impermanent.

But scholars have differing opinions on this process. Künkhyen Jamyang Shepa states that for those with very sharp intelligence, positive arguments are not required.[33] Rather, absurd consequences themselves are enough for sharp opponents to gain the correct insight into emptiness. Many follow Jamyang Shepa in this view. This is the origin of the term *prāsaṅgika*, which is back-translated from the Tibetan *thal 'gyur ba*, or "proponents of absurd consequences." A Prāsaṅgika is thus a wielder of reductio arguments. A Svātantrika (*Rang rgyud pa*), on the other hand, is one who propounds his own argument for a thesis. The proponents of these positions are sometimes called in English *consequentialist* and *autonomist*, respectively.

In *Fundamental Verses on the Middle Way*, chapter 1, verse 1, Nāgārjuna writes:

1. Neither from itself, nor from another,
nor from both, nor without a cause
is anything, anywhere, at any time,
ever produced.

Here Nāgārjuna introduces the structure of the argument, whereas in the rest of the chapter he develops the absurd consequences.

The *probandum*, or thesis, what needs to be proven beyond a shadow of doubt, is that things do not have intrinsic production. The reasoning is that they are not produced either from themselves, from others, from both, or from neither.

The first line in Tibetan reads thusly:

*Dag las ma yin . . .*
Neither from itself . . .

This means "not produced from itself." The Sāṃkhya school of Indian philosophy believes that things like sprouts cannot arise unless they already exist at the time of their causes; they believe the effects exist within the causes in an unmanifested way. Thus for the Sāṃkhyas, things do not arise from other distinct things but from causes that share identical nature with it. This first line exposes the absurd consequence that if something were produced from itself, then it must be produced again and again. The cause would be repeating itself in perpetuity, thus falling into an infinite regress. A seed would perpetuate until the end of time. Therefore, it could never be the case that such things as a sprout would not arise again; once arisen it would have to arise again. This also means the cause would never finish, so the effect could never be produced. These are the absurd consequences that follow from self-production.

The critique of self-production leading to the debate between Prāsaṅgikas and Svātantrikas begins with the following gloss of this verse by Buddhapālita:

> Things do not arise from themselves, because their arising would be pointless. An infinite regress of arising would follow.[34]

Bhāviveka reviewed a shorter and a longer version of this reasoning from Buddhapālita. The verse above is the shorter version, which Bhāviveka chose to criticize; he had no issue with the longer version. The criticism levied by Bhāviveka against Buddhapālita, and Candrakīrti's response defending Buddhapālita, is referred to in Tibetan as *theldog* (*thal bzlog*) or "reversing the same style argument back onto the opponent."

If something were to arise intrinsically from itself, it would be pointless and would continually arise again. This is Buddhapālita's position. In his shorter version, "arising again" is not explicitly mentioned. Bhāviveka was challenging Buddhapālita's rejection of self-arising posited by Sāṃkhya philosophy. Bhāviveka gives three reasons: (1) he has not given valid reasoning, (2) he has not given a valid example to support that reasoning, and (3) Buddhapālita has not properly challenged Sāṃkhya's position.

The Sāṃkhya position is basically that the result and the cause are of the same nature. It is commonly agreed that a result arises from a cause. The Sāṃkhyas posit that cause, effect, and everything are simply manifestations of the "universal principle" (Skt. *pradhan* or *prakṛti*; Tib. *spyi gtso bo*), and that a result arises from a cause that shares the nature.

Furthermore, according to the Sāṃkhya position there are two kinds of results: one manifest, the other unmanifested. In the case of the manifest result, according to Bhāviveka, the Sāṃkhyas would respond that they do not accept a manifest result arising from causes having the same nature as itself. In the case of the unmanifested result, the Sāṃkhyas would respond that if an unmanifested result is not arisen from a cause of identical nature, then nothing could arise. Whatever reasoning Buddhapālita would assert to challenge the Sāṃkhya position would according to Bhāviveka actually imply the direct opposite of the predicate. This means it could only imply that the unmanifested result would arise from itself. The subject here is "unmanifested result"; the predicate is "not arising from itself" (*itself* refers to cause and result with identical nature). The opposite of the predicate is "arising from itself." The reason is "it is pointless" and an "infinite regress" would follow.

Bhāviveka says to Buddhapālita that what he says is not consistent with reasoning. Literally, the subject (impermanent things), the predicate (not arising from themselves), the reason (arising has no point and would be infinite regress) are what has been stated. If this is the case, then the reason (arising would be pointless and endless) does not exist conventionally. Something that does not exist conventionally cannot be used as a reason to refute others.

If, on the other hand, the implication drawn is to be accepted as the argument, then it would include the reason "if there is self-arising, it would be pointless" and "endless." If this were the case, then for the Sāṃkhya when the reason is set forth, they would have understood "no arising from self." When the reason is understood, the predicate would also have been understood. Yet logically, the reason is understood first, before drawing the conclusion (predicate). This would absurdly imply that the Sāṃkhyas would have understood what Buddhapālita was trying to negate: that is, the absence of arising from self.

Bhāviveka said that Buddhapālita's negation of self-arising is not consistent. Therefore, the only thing left for Buddhapālita to say is that there is a purpose and end to arising. Although this is what he meant to say, he did not say this directly. He wants to imply arising, while at the same time negating self-arising. When the predicate is understood in the subject, absence of self-arising is understood. At the same time, Buddhapālita wants to imply arising, since he says there is a purpose to arising and an end to arising. If this is implied, then the absence of self-arising becomes an affirming negative. This contradicts the Madhyamaka philosophy that asserts the absence of self-arising is a nonaffirming negative.

To recap, the four contradictions found by Bhāviveka in Buddhapālita are these: there is no valid reasoning, there is no valid example, he has not refuted the Sāṃkhya position properly, and his own position is not consistent with Madhyamaka philosophy.

Candrakīrti, in defense of Buddhapālita, finds the same faults in Bhāviveka that he (Bhāviveka) finds in Buddhapālita. This is exactly the meaning of *theldog*.

Tsongkhapa continues the argument in his *Ocean of Reasoning*:

In response to this Bhāviveka alleges that this does not make any sense, because this argument provides neither reasoning nor an example to prove the non-existence of arising from self. Therefore it merely states the thesis.

He says that because Buddhapālita does not examine their thesis he does not dispel the errors they commit, saying that if the meaning of "from self" according to the Sāṃkhya were *from the manifested effect of itself* then that would be to establish that which has already been established. If on the other hand it meant *from an unmanifested cause itself* then everything that is arisen would arise that way. And this would be inconsistent.

He also says it does not make sense because the argument is open to dispute from another opponent. . . .

Here is how Candrakīrti refutes these allegations. The absurd consequence that shows that there is a contradiction between further arising having a point and its existence can refute arising from self. If it could not, then even presenting autonomous arguments could not refute it. Therefore, there is no need to present autonomous arguments or examples. Since it makes no sense for mādhyamikas to propound autonomous arguments, there is no need to rebut charges others make regarding autonomous premises or autonomous conclusions.[35]

Bhāviveka argues that Buddhapālita must use autonomous examples, premises, and conclusions that are accepted by the opponent in order to eliminate their mistaken view. Similarly, Candrakīrti says that Mādhyamikas should rebut others' arguments only by showing that their arguments lead to absurd consequences in their own right. They should not propound their own contrary arguments, as to do so requires the presumption that the Mādhyamika and the opponent can accept common premises. But they can't, he argues, because the opponent takes the meaning of the premise to encode intrinsic nature and substantial existence, and the Mādhyamika merely conventional reality. So, they have no commonly accepted subjects; so, the Mādhyamika cannot mount an autonomous argument.[36]

The second half of the first line reads thus:

*. . . gzhan las min*
. . . nor from another

This means not produced from another. If something were to be produced from another, then it could be produced by things unrelated to it, even causally. This is because both causes and noncauses are *other*. But this also makes no sense, for how could something be produced from something that is not its cause? If it could, then anything could produce anything in this strange fantasy world of intrinsic existence. This is the refutation of production from another that Buddhapālita cites in his treatise *Commentary to the Fundamental Treatise of the Middle Way* (*Buddhapālitamūlamadhyamakavṛtti*). Candrakīrti uses this same argument in his *Entering the Middle Way*. The main point here is this: if the cause and effect were intrinsically other, they would be completely unrelated. This would contradict their standing in a causal relation.

The first half of the second line in Tibetan reads thus:

*Gnyis las ma yin ...*
**Nor from both ...**

Things are not produced from both self and other. The Sāṃkhyas posit that the sprout arising from a seed is actually arising from itself, but it's arising from conditions they assert to be arising from other. In this way they accept production from both self and other. The Jains also believe in production from both self and other. They assert the arising of a clay pot is arising from self in terms of the clay, whereas it arises from other regarding the potter and his wheel. While it is true that a potter, a wheel, and clay are all necessary to make a pot, none of their contributions amount to intrinsic production. This is because each of them individually cannot make a pot; it requires the mutual help of each one to make a pot. Relationship precludes intrinsic production.

Production from both self and other has already been refuted based on the arguments presented individually refuting production from self and refuting production from other.

The second half of the second line reads in Tibetan:

> ... *rgyu med min*
> ... **nor without a cause**

This means there is no production without a cause. The Lokāyata, the materialist school of Indian philosophy, argued that there is no causation at all, and that things simply arise by chance. But this position is refuted because if things could arise without a cause, then anything could arise from anything. Thus all efforts would be pointless, for there would be no consistent results.

The next two lines, which explain the first two lines, read in Tibetan:

> *dngos po gang dag gang na yang*
> *skye ba nam yang yod ma yin*
> **is anything, anywhere, at any time,**
> **ever produced**

This means that intrinsic production whatsoever is completely and utterly impossible. Tsongkhapa's *Ocean of Reasoning* explains that such intrinsic production is always impossible, whatsoever at any time, at any place, or in any doctrine or view. This statement by Tsongkhapa echoes the conclusion of the previous two lines of this first verse of *Fundamental Verses on the Middle Way*.

Things have no production from themselves at all. Things have no intrinsic production from others. Likewise, things have no production from both themselves and others at all. Lastly, things have no production without a cause at all.

Literally, the verse must be taken like this: its explicit meaning does not prove lack of intrinsic production of things, but that things have no production from these four alternatives. Yet *implicitly* this verse establishes no intrinsic production. This is the main point of this first chapter. For just like in the Buddha's prajñāpāramitā sūtras, the adjective *intrinsic* is often left out, but its meaning is always there. Thus *no intrinsic production* is the conclusion Nāgārjuna repeatedly establishes in this first chapter, "Analysis of Conditions."

There are of course sources for this explanation coming from the teachings of the Buddha. In many different Mahāyāna sūtras there is mention of things not being produced from themselves, others, both, or neither. For instance, Nāgārjuna's *Fundamental Verses on the Middle Way* resonates well with the prajñāpāramitā sūtras. And Candrakīrti in his *Clear Words* refers to a sūtra that discusses no production from the perspective of the tetralemma.

## The Second Section: Refutation of the Four Conditions

Those who reify reality argue that things have intrinsic production and intrinsic existence in general, because in the sūtras we find mention of four conditions by which things are produced. The first section of chapter 1 of *Fundamental Verses on the Middle Way* focuses on refuting causes and conditions in general. This second section refutes each of the four conditions individually.

The second verse reads thusly:

2. **There are four conditions:**
**the causal, the objective,**
**the proximate, and the dominant.**
**There is no fifth condition.**

The four conditions—the causal, the objective, the proximate, and the dominant—at first glance are a bit abstract. In order to explain them, we can look at the example from the introduction: the color blue. In this analogy, blue color is the objective condition. The visual faculty, which is the sense faculty that allows us to see color, similar to the eyeball although not identical to it, is the dominant condition. The mental consciousness immediately preceding the visual faculty that induces the visual consciousness is the proximate condition. The latent potential for the production of the visual consciousness perceiving the color blue is the causal condition. This illustration is according to a Yogācāra understanding.

In order for the visual consciousness to perceive the color blue it depends upon these four conditions. Yet for those who reify reality, the fact that a visual consciousness perceiving the color blue has these four conditions establishes things to exist intrinsically. Nāgārjuna argues that because things are produced in dependence upon these four conditions, they *cannot* exist intrinsically. Nāgārjuna maintains that because things are produced in dependence on these four conditions, therefore these four are in fact conditions. If the visual consciousness perceiving the color blue was not produced in dependence on these four conditions, it would make no sense to call these four *conditions*.

> 3. An intrinsic nature of things
> does not exist in its conditions, etc.
> If the entity that is self does not exist,
> the entity that is other does not exist.

In the sūtras, the Buddha did teach four conditions for the production of phenomena, but these were taught on a conventional level, not on an ultimate level. Thus the four conditions do exist conventionally, but not ultimately. Therefore, the sūtras do not demonstrate intrinsic production. Nor do they demonstrate intrinsic conditions for production.

## Refutation of an Intrinsic Causal Condition

In *Ocean of Reasoning,* Tsongkhapa comments on this verse, stating if things had intrinsic production, then the effect would necessarily be in the cause. This is because if the *act of production* (not the effect itself) were in the cause, then that which is produced, the effect, would also have to be in the cause. If the effect were produced intrinsically, then the effect would have the power to give rise to itself. The effect would arise all the time and thus be there all the time. Hence, it would have to be there at the time of the cause.

The Prāsaṅgika school explains that if things were produced intrinsically, it would mean that the effect would exist independently. Therefore, how could it not be there at the time of the cause? Since an intrinsically produced effect would be present at all times, it would have to be present at the time of the cause.

Verses 4–6 read thusly:

**4. An action does not have conditions;
no action exists without conditions.**

Although there are no conditions without an
  action,
[conditions] do have an action still.

5. They are *called* conditions by virtue
of something arising in dependence on them.
When nothing arises [in dependence] on them,
how can they not be called nonconditions?

6. Even in regard to nonexistent or existent objects
the condition is untenable.
Because if nonexistent, what would it be the
  condition of?
If existent, what is the need for a condition?

Verse five explains that conditions are conditions by virtue of something arising in dependence on them. Intrinsic
production contradicts this statement. Nāgārjuna argues
that if things were produced intrinsically, the effect would
be independent, hence unrelated and not present at the
time of the cause. Yet, an intrinsically real effect must be
present at all times, thus also at the time of the cause.

To this contradiction, the Grammarians offer a rebuttal positing an intermediary, called an *action of producing
an effect*, between the cause and the effect. The Grammarians, a non-Buddhist school, argue that if an effect were to
be produced directly by a cause, then this might be true, but

that it is not the case; an effect is not produced directly by a cause. The Grammarians claim that, when analyzed more carefully, the cause produces the action of producing an effect. When the action producing an effect is produced, the cause ceases. Therefore, it is the action of production that produces the effect, and not the cause itself. Thus, there is no direct production from the cause. Therefore, for the reason that there is an intermediary in the chain of production, the effect itself is not present at the time of the cause.

Nāgārjuna takes issue with the Grammarians. First he explains their view as he sees it, and then he refutes it. According to the Grammarians, the action of producing an effect must exist intrinsically. If it did exist intrinsically, then why would that action of producing the effect not be present at the time of the cause? And if the action were there at the time of the cause, then why would the effect not also be there at the time of the cause? Furthermore, the Grammarians would not assert that there is some action producing an effect that is not produced by a condition or cause. For these reasons, whatever activities there are at any time at any place, they must all be produced from causes and conditions. If there were actions not produced from causes and conditions—that is, causeless production—then anything could cause anything. This would be senseless. Therefore, Nāgārjuna states that whatever actions there are, they must all come from causes and conditions.

If production existed intrinsically, would the effect exist at the time of the cause, or would the effect not exist at the time of the cause? If the effect was not there at the time of the cause, then the effect could not exist at any time. An intrinsically existent effect either never exists or always exists. Thus, if the effect is not there at the time of the cause, it cannot exist at any time. Therefore, what purpose would the cause serve? On the other hand, if the effect were present at the time of the cause, then what purpose would the cause serve? Since the effect would already be there, the cause would be impotent. It would serve no purpose, for it would not be needed to produce the effect. It would have nothing to do. Thus, the absurd consequence from postulating intrinsic production would be that there is no relationship at all between the cause and effect. Therefore, the cause would have absolutely nothing to do with the effect. Nāgārjuna concludes that the causal condition cannot exist intrinsically.

## Refutation of an Intrinsic Objective Condition

Nāgārjuna then refutes the intrinsic objective condition. The logic he uses is the same as in the previous, causal condition. Here Nāgārjuna asks whether the visual consciousness exists at the time of its objective condition. If the visual consciousness were simultaneous with the objective condition, it could not cause vision. If it occurred before the objective condition, then it is not what is presently seen.

Verses 7 and 8 read:

7. When a phenomenon is neither established
as existent, nonexistent, nor both,
how could that which establishes be called a cause?
**If that is the case, [a causal condition] is unfeasible.**

8. [You] have emphatically stated an existent
entity
[mind] has no object.
**If this entity [mind] has no object,
how can an object of perception be possible?**

## *Refutation of an Intrinsic Proximate Condition*

Following this we have the refutation of the proximate condition. The proximate condition is a condition existing immediately prior to its effect. As soon as the effect is produced, it ceases. The proximate condition requires a process of ceasing.

There are two declinations of the Tibetan term *'gag*, present and past tense, each with a slightly different spelling but the same pronunciation. The verb without a *sa* at the end (*'gag*) means "ceasing." On the other hand, the verb with the *sa* (*'gags*) means *has ceased*. The latter means that something has already ceased. However, the former means something is in the process of ceasing, which means it gradually ceases, over a period of time—which would be impossible if it were to exist intrinsically.

Gradual ceasing requires a series of cause-and-effect relationships, which is contradictory to existing intrinsically. Therefore, prior to the effect, the cause must have already ceased. There could be no process of ceasing, since it would have already ceased before producing its effect. Therefore, the effect could not be produced directly from its cause since there would be a gap between the cessation of the cause and the production of its effect. This argument regarding cessation is more fully explained in chapter 7, "Analysis of Arising, Enduring, and Ceasing," particularly verses 26 and 27:

26. That which has ceased does not cease.
What has not yet ceased does not cease.
Nor does that which is in the process of ceasing.
What nonarisen can cease?

27. The cessation of an entity that
is enduring is not tenable.
Nor is the cessation of an
entity that is not enduring.

If impermanence existed intrinsically, then only three alternatives are possible: (1) That which has ceased does not cease because the past and the present are contradictory. This is because the present activity of cessation and the past disintegration are contradictory. Furthermore, that which has already ceased has completed cessation and thus does not need to cease again; (2) that which has not yet ceased cannot cease because it has not yet arisen; (3) nor can that which is in the process of ceasing cease. This is because intrinsic cessation would have two activities of cessation—the activity of ceasing and the cessation of the subject that is ceasing. Therefore, intrinsic existent impermanence is impossible.

The ninth verse of chapter 1 reads thusly:

9. **If phenomena do not arise,**
**cessation becomes unfeasible.**
**Therefore, a proximate [condition] is untenable.**
**If things have ceased, what then is a condition?**

What has immediately ceased cannot be the proximate cause of what has immediately arisen. This is because prior to production of a result, such as a sprout, the ceasing of the cause, such as a seed, is untenable. If the seed has already ceased before the production, then how could the ceasing of the seed before the production of the sprout act as a proximate cause of the production of the sprout? This is because there would be no seed immediately before the arising of the sprout. If the ceasing of the seed is a proximate cause of the unborn sprout, this is also untenable since the ceasing of the seed and the arising of the sprout are simultaneous. Thus, at the time of the ceasing of the seed, the sprout is not unborn but arising.

If the ceasing of the cause (for example, a seed) that occurs after the production of the result is said to be its proximate cause, then how could it be the proximate cause when the activity of production is already over, as it would occur later?

If the act of ceasing and the act of production, which are simultaneous, are said to be each other's proximate cause, then for an intrinsic cause and an intrinsic result, at the time of the action of production of the sprout, the sprout must be there. Likewise, at the time of the action of ceasing of the seed, the seed must be there. This makes the seed and the sprout simultaneous with the act of ceasing the seed and the act of producing the sprout, since there is no time difference. Thus, for intrinsic production of a sprout and intrinsic cessation of a seed, which is the agent, the sprout and seed must exist simultaneously with the action of producing and ceasing. This is because an intrinsic action of production and an intrinsic action of arising are devoid of any dependence.

## *Refutation of an Intrinsic Dominant Condition*

Those who reify reality and the Prāsaṅgika Mādhyamikas use the same reason to different ends: production from causes and conditions. Those who reify reality use this argument to prove intrinsic existence. The Prāsaṅgikas use the argument of production dependent on causes and conditions to prove there is no intrinsic existence.

The dominant condition refers to the sense faculty, which is quintessential for the result. While a sense faculty is similar to a sense organ, such as the eye, it is not exactly the same, though "an internal physical entity with clarity" is still difficult for us to fathom.

In general we could say if something exists, then something else arises. And if that something does not exist, then that something else does not arise. This shows the important role of the dominant condition in the arising of the result. Take for example the color blue. With an intact eye sense faculty, the color blue can be seen. But without an intact eye sense faculty the color blue cannot be perceptually seen.

Verse 10 reads thusly:

10. **Since there is no existence in things
lacking intrinsic nature,
the statement "because this exists, that arises"
is not acceptable.**

Since all phenomena arise dependently, all phenomena lack intrinsic existence. Therefore, it is untenable to say that either the cause ("by this existing") or the effect ("that comes to be") exists intrinsically. Furthermore, if things were not nonintrinsically existent—that is, if they were intrinsically existent—then production in dependence on causes and conditions would be impossible.

## The Third Section: Refutation of an Effect

The first chapter of Nāgārjuna's *Fundamental Verses on the Middle Way* presents many types of reasoning. It methodically analyzes and refutes intrinsic causes and conditions and the full array of arguments presented by those who think that to exist is to be nonempty and to be empty is not to exist. As we have discussed before, those who reify reality believe that production must intrinsically exist because there are causes and conditions for their arising—these four conditions taught by the Buddha that produce all phenomena.

Moreover, if there were no production, as those who reify reality interpret the Prāsaṅgika position argue, then causes and conditions would be meaningless. Yet the Buddha explained causes and conditions repeatedly in his teachings. Furthermore, for those who reify reality, no intrinsic production is tantamount to no production at all. They continue arguing that things must be intrinsically existent, because we experience things being produced and ceasing, enduring and disintegrating, coming and going, and being identical and different. From this analysis and reflection they gain confidence that for things to exist they must exist intrinsically.

Using many logical arguments, Nāgārjuna systematically refutes an intrinsic objective condition, causal condition, proximate condition, and dominant condition. Those who reify reality respond defensively. Maybe these four conditions do not exist intrinsically. Nevertheless, there still must exist a conventional condition. We see thread made into cloth. We see a seed grow into a sprout. We see wood combust into fire. These examples demonstrate for those who reify reality that there is actually something called a condition.

The arguments so far have concentrated on conditions. Now Nāgārjuna turns his attention to effects, arguing with similar logic.

11. The effect is not in the conditions
individually or collectively.
Thus how could something not in
the conditions be produced from them?

12. However, despite the result being nonexistent
[in the conditions]

**if it arises from these conditions,
why would it not arise
from nonconditions?**

In verse 11 the problem of why this particular effect arises from these conditions is addressed. Candrakīrti discusses this with the example of a cloth that is woven from threads, loom, shuttle, weaver, and so on. The cloth is not in the conditions individually; it is not found in the threads, the loom, the weaver, and so on. If the cloth were in each of the conditions, then as there are many conditions, so too would there be many cloths. Nor is the cloth in the collection of conditions, for it is not in each of the individual parts that form the collection. When we speak of the individual parts before the formation of the whole "cloth," then they become conditions for the cloth. However, if we are to think of parts that exist simultaneously with the cloth, then they are not conditions because conditions and result do not abide at the same time. However, their previous moments that added together to form the whole "cloth" are conditions.

In verse 12 Nāgārjuna argues that if the effect and its conditions are distinct, the effect would also be able to be produced from those things that are not its causes and conditions as well. This follows the argument against production from other, which we have already discussed.

13. If the effect had the nature of the conditions,
conditions would not have their own nature.
How can an effect (which arises) from that which
lacks
its own self-entity be in the nature of conditions?

The effect is distinct from the causes and conditions yet it arises from them; it consists in them or is composed of them. This is the view of the Nyāya (Tib. Rigpachen) school of Indian philosophy, a non-Buddhist school whose name means "followers of logic." The example is once again of threads that make up a piece of cloth. Āryadeva's *Four Hundred Verses* (*Catuḥśataka*) says this in chapter 14, verse 13:

Cloth comes into existence from causes.
The causes come into existence from others.
How could something that does not exist on
its own give rise to something else?[37]

As we've seen, the Sāṃkhyas maintain the effect is preexistent in the causes and conditions. It is not tenable for them that anything, such as a sprout, could arise unless it already existed at the time of its cause. Hence effects exist in their causes in an unmanifested way. Nāgārjuna refutes this by saying that there would then be no point to arising; there would be no point in a sprout arising again since it has already arisen. Therefore, things such as a sprout would arise endlessly in an infinite regress.

The Sāṃkhyas could respond that an unmanifested potential entity must arise for it to be manifest. Furthermore, once it has arisen, there is no need for it to arise again. But there is still this problem: if the manifested was already present, there is no need for it to arise, and if it arose having existed previously, then it must continually arise in an infinite regress. If the Sāṃkhyas then argue the manifested did not exist previously, then they have changed their position regarding the effect being present in the causes and conditions.

In the thirteenth verse Nāgārjuna draws the conclusion that since causes and conditions do not exist intrinsically, their effects also do not exist intrinsically. If the effects are not produced intrinsically, they must be produced dependently. Therefore, the effect cannot be in the nature of the cause, since the cause has no nature. The Sāṃkhyas respond that although the effect and the cause are not of the same nature, nevertheless they do exist separately as intrinsically existent things.

Verse 14 reads thusly:

**14.  Therefore, there is no result that is of
the nature of the conditions or nonconditions.
And since the result is nonexistent,**

**how can something be [its] condition or noncondition?**

Nāgārjuna gives a final response in the fourteenth verse, the last verse of chapter 1, and the Sāṃkhyas retreat from their position. If the effect does not exist in the cause, then the cause could never produce the effect.

As verse 13 explained, the effect cannot be made up of its conditions. The conclusion then would be that the effect must be made up of nonconditions; if the cloth is not made of thread, then it might be made of paper, which is the condition for a book, but a noncondition for cloth. This makes no sense. Thus, we are left unable to establish a real effect. And if we cannot establish a real effect, then how can we establish a real condition or even a real noncondition?

As the Buddha said in the *Jewel Mine Sūtra* (*Ratnākara Sūtra*):

Whatever is empty and cannot be perceived is like the tracks of a bird in the expanse of the sky.[38]

The Buddha teaches insight into reality, which is free of fabrications.

All phenomena are immutable and stable; unchangeable, without turmoil and peaceful,

just as empty space is not seen.[39]
The ignorant are confused about this.[40]

Reality is empty. And again the Buddha teaches:

Phenomena are neither born nor come into existence;
nor die, nor transform, nor age.
The lion among men has shown this and led
hundreds of sentient beings to see this.[41]

Nothing is intrinsically born and nothing intrinsically dies. The Buddha led many to this realization of reality, leading the way for others who are qualified to do the same.

## Emptiness and Dependent Arising

The key elements in Nāgārjuna's *Fundamental Verses on the Middle Way* are emptiness and its identical twin, dependent arising.

Regarding emptiness, the crucial point for practice and for understanding is recognizing the mistaken trap we continually fall into that perpetuates the vicious cycle of discontent: the assumption that appearances have real, objective references. This is why it is so crucial to precisely identify the object of negation; once that is done, half the battle is won. Then it requires meditating on its negation.

It's important to note that merely not finding anything on analysis is not the realization of emptiness.

We do not find a chariot when analyzing the chariot in terms of its shape, parts, wheels, and so on, nor when analyzing it separate from the parts, but that is not the realization of emptiness. It *leads to* the realization of emptiness. To realize emptiness is to realize that the thing we sought is in principle unfindable, and to cease reifying it. When we critically search for the designated object within or outside the basis of designation, we do not find it. However, if we try to find a thing without critically searching for it, we can find it. Finding a chariot outside the chariot, for example, on the road, and finding a chariot within a chariot are two ways of finding a chariot. The first is finding a chariot through "the analysis into conventional nature" (*tha snyad dpyod byed kyi rigs pa*). Here, we only search for something that is conventionally known as a chariot. The second is finding a chariot through the analysis into ultimate nature (*don dam dpyod byed kyi rigs pa*). Here we search for an objective chariot, either within a chariot or outside of it. Thus, objects are findable conventionally but unfindable ultimately.

In *Essence of Eloquent Interpretation* Tsongkhapa states that because we do not find the chariot through analysis, and because it is designated dependently, therefore we conclude that it is empty of self-existence from in and of itself.[42] When we first investigate the designated object, we cannot find it. This implies the designated object is imputed contingent upon its basis of designation. Due to this reason of dependence, we come to the conclusion that there is no inherent existence.

When one realizes emptiness free from intrinsic existence correctly, that is, not nothingness, it induces a strong conviction in our understanding of conventional reality. When one realizes emptiness, it is through negating the correct object of negation. Thereby perception is freed from reification. As one's certainty in conventional reality deepens, the yoke of the extreme of nihilism is freed.

In this way understanding emptiness complements and enhances our understanding of conventional reality. Similarly, understanding illusory-like conventional reality complements and enhances our understanding of emptiness. These two truths are mutually supportive. When one realizes conventional existence, that in turn induces greater certainty in the understanding of emptiness. Thus, the two truths go together hand in hand and are mutually supportive, mutually dependent, and mutually enhancing. All phenomena naturally possess these two ontological (or existential) qualities known as the two truths.

The other key element is dependent arising.

In *Ocean of Reasoning*, Tsongkhapa breaks down the

statement that effects are produced in dependence on causes. He points out that the word *dependence* demonstrates the lack of intrinsic existence. On the other hand, the word *produced* demonstrates the lack of nonexistence, as it upholds the existence of things.

Chone Rinpoché[43] has written a commentary on Tsongkhapa's *In Praise of Dependent Origination* called *Commentary Interspersed with Tsongkhapa's Root Text* (*Spel mar bstod pa*). In it, Chone Rinpoché comments that the word *rten*, "dependent," does not contradict emptiness. Rather it implies no *intrinsic* existence. The word *'byung ba*, "origination" or "birth," indicates acceptance of worldly convention. If the result and the cause both existed intrinsically, then the result could not depend on the cause. Likewise, the cause could not depend on the result. Thereby they would be totally independent and unrelated. In this way all the refutations of the Prāsaṅgika view are turned back on the opponents.

When we analyze production, nothing is found that can actually be pointed to as an effect. The Tibetan word for "production," *skye ba*, also means "birth" or "origination." If birth existed as it appears, we must be able to find it when we investigate. But we cannot find it. We cannot precisely identify birth. As nothing from its own side can be identified, this leads to the conclusion that birth is projected from the side of the mind, from thought. Since production is projected by thought in dependence on many factors, Tsongkhapa tells us that the argument from dependent origination proves that production does not exist intrinsically from its own side.

In *Ocean of Reasoning*, Tsongkapa closes his commentary on chapter 1 of *The Fundamental Verses on the Middle Way* by warning against falling into either extreme of nihilism and reification, and he bolsters his argument with pellucid words from the Buddha, Candrakīrti, and Buddhapālita.

First, he points us to Candrakīrti, saying that according to his *Clear Words*, such statements as "dependent origination is free of cessation, and free of production," which is from the salutation verses at the beginning of chapter 1, refute ultimate arising but do not refute conventional arising.[44]

Next, Tsongkhapa refers to a line from the *Descent into Laṅkā Sūtra* quoted in Candrakīrti's *Clear Words*:

I have said that all things are nonarisen meaning that they are essentially nonarisen.[45]

Tsongkhapa goes on to quote Buddhapālita twice. First, he draws from the beginning of the first chapter of *Buddhapālitamūlamadhyamakavṛtti*:

To say that something arises is merely convention.

Then from the end of that same chapter:

> To say that something arises is to say that it merely
> exists conventionally.[46]

Finally, Tsongkhapa echoes the conventional nature
of reality:

> Then, since the benefits and harms of causes
> and effects are undeniable, one should develop
> ascertainment, thinking as follows: "Although in
> the context of mere imputation, causes give rise to
> effects, it is erroneous for me to grasp them in the
> context of existence through their own characteris-
> tics." One should not allow this to undermine one's
> ascertainment of the dependent arising of causes
> and effects.[47]

Thus it is very clear from words of the Buddha, Buddhapālita, Candrakīrti, and Tsongkhapa, and echoed in
Nāgārjuna's works, that when we say that all phenomena
are nonarisen and nonannihilated, we mean *ultimately*
not arisen and *ultimately* not annihilated. Conventionally phenomena still arise and are still annihilated. Otherwise the ethical behavior of nonharm and the view of
no-self from the Buddha's quintessential teachings would
make no sense.

A fitting end to this chapter also comes from a line from Tsongkhapa's *Ocean of Reasoning*:

> So these arguments in the first chapter should be understood as the *eye* through which all of the scriptures that present nonarising in this and similar ways can be seen.[48]

# Conclusion

In this book, we've examined Nāgārjuna's *Fundamental Verses on the Middle Way* according to the schema used by His Holiness the Dalai Lama. First, in Nāgārjuna's chapter 26, we examined the twelve links of dependent origination to learn why and how we cycle through saṃsāra. Then, with chapter 18, we discovered that there is no inherent self that cycles. Then we studied chapter 24, which analyzes the four noble truths, to reestablish conventional reality—there still is samsara fueled by ignorance, and release in nirvana fueled by the wisdom of emptiness. Next, chapter 22 presented an investigation of the Tathāgata and we learned that even emptiness is empty. Finally, Nāgārjuna's chapter 1 reemphasizes that emptiness is pervasive.

This book only addresses five of the twenty-seven chapters in Nāgārjuna's treatise. We have only scratched the surface, but it has been a scratch guided by Tsongkhapa and by His Holiness the Dalai Lama and the scholars on whom he relies. The other chapters are worth reading, and I recommend that the interested reader continue with the study of Nāgārjuna's text, a study that is always richly rewarding. Those chapters address virtually every topic of importance in Buddhist philosophy—the self as subject of experience, agency, perception, liberation, arising and cessation, suffering, and many others—applying the analysis that demonstrates that phenomena are empty of intrinsic nature in each case.

Production itself, the things produced, and the causes for their production are all empty. Yet conventionally, as dependent phenomena and events, they do exist. There is on the conventional level *dukkha* (Skt. *duḥkha*; Tib. *sdug bsngal*), suffering, with its causes. And because there are causes, we can eliminate dukkha through the wisdom of emptiness.

In order to do this, however, we must adopt these principles in our hearts and incorporate them into our lives; we can't just leave them on the intellectual level. When Jeffrey Hopkins, esteemed scholar and friend, was a young man, his first teacher, Geshé Wangyal, gave him some pith advice. He told Jeffrey to label whatever he saw as "false." So Jeffrey went around saying to himself, "Door, false; table, false; reflection of Jeffrey's face in the mirror, false; glass of wine, false; mother, false; my teacher Geshé Wangyal, false." In this way Hopkins practiced seeing himself and the world as like an illusion. This is a very practical way to begin to see through the mistake of taking everything as real and solid. Nothing is as it appears.

This practice must not only be for the wellbeing and happiness of ourselves; it must be to benefit all living beings. Our motivation needs to mature and become as vast as the heavens. We are just one, whereas others are countless. To be only concerned with the benefit of number one, while countless beings live in misery, is not only foolish and immature; it is downright selfish. This is like putting your head in the sand to block out the rest of the world. A wider scope is imperative, even for our own survival. We are all interconnected.

# APPENDIX

## Twenty Verses on Bodhicitta from Nāgārjuna's *Precious Advice for a King*

66. Honoring in all ways the buddhas,
the Dharma, the community, and also
the bodhisattvas, to them I go for refuge,
and pay homage to those worthy of homage.

67. I turn away from all negativity
and embrace all kinds of merit;
I rejoice in all the merit
(amassed by) all sentient beings.

68. With bowed head and palms together
I beseech all perfect buddhas
to turn the wheel of Dharma and
remain as long as beings remain.

69. Through the merit of doing this and
the merit I have done and not yet done,
may all sentient beings be endowed
with unsurpassable bodhicitta.

70. May all sentient beings have immaculate
faculties and transcend the freedomless [states];
may they control their own actions
and live by a good livelihood.

71. May all embodied beings have jewels
in their hands, and may a limitless [amount]
of all kinds of necessities remain
inexhaustible for as long as saṃsāra endures.

72. At all times may all women
become supreme persons.
May all beings be endowed
with intelligence and legs.

73. May all beings have a good complexion
and also a good physique. May they be radiant
and pleasant to behold. Free of illness,
may they be strong and live long.

74. May they all gain expertise in the methods
and become free of all suffering.

May they become devoted to the Three Jewels
and have the great treasure of Buddhadharma.

75. May they be adorned with love, compassion, joy,
[the ability to] remain equanimous in the face of
     hardship,
generosity, morality, patience, heroic effort,
meditative concentration, and wisdom.

76. Thus adorned, may they complete all the
     collections,
and [obtaining] brilliant marks and secondary
     signs,
may they traverse without hindrance
the ten stages [to] the inconceivable.

77–78. May I also become adorned with
these good qualities and all others as well;
may I become freed from all faults
and may I attain supreme love for all beings;
may I perfect the virtues
to which all beings aspire
and may I always dispel the suffering
of all embodied beings.

79. In all worlds may all beings
who are feeling anxious due to fear

become completely fearless
merely by hearing my name.

80–81. From seeing and thinking of me,
and from merely hearing my name,
may beings become clear minded,
undisturbed, and at ease;
may it be definite that they will awaken;
and in all their future lives,
may they attain the five psychic powers.
In all ways may I always do what brings
benefit and happiness to all beings.

82. May I always dissuade all at once
all those beings of any world
who intend to engage in negativity,
without doing them any harm.

83. Like the earth, water, wind, and fire,
medicinal herbs, and the trees of the wilderness,
may I always be made use of freely
by all beings just as they wish.

84. May I be beloved of beings, and may they
be more beloved to me than myself.
May I bear the results of their negativity,
and may they have the results of all my virtue.

85.  As long as there is some single
sentient being somewhere who is not yet free,
may I remain [in the world] for that being's sake,
Even if I have attained unexcelled awakening.

# COLOPHON

This book was based in its early stages on the oral verse-by-verse teachings of Gen Namgyal Wangchen of Drepung Loseling Monastery. The oral translation, for most of these teachings, was done by Tenzin Tsepag. Research, adding sections, and substantial editing and re-editing was done by Barry Kerzin, the simple monk Tenzin Choerab, over a period of time spanning more than ten years.

May His Holiness the Fourteenth Dalai Lama remain healthy, live a long life, and succeed in all of his enlightened activities. Through this work may all sentient beings submerged in the waves of oceans of existence travel on the path trodden by the supreme leader of the bipeds.

Mundgod,
Dharamsala,
Whitefish, Montana

# NOTES

1. *Geshé* (*dge bshes*, short for *dge ba'i bshes gnyen*) means "virtuous friend." It is a title conferred in the Tibetan Buddhist scholastic tradition after years of rigorous study; in Tibet the geshé curriculum spanned over twenty years, but it has been significantly shortened in India. The curriculum includes five topics: Abhidharma (higher knowledge), Prajñāpāramitā (perfection of wisdom), Madhyamaka (wisdom of the middle way, as in the title of Nāgārjuna's text), Pramāṇa (logic), and Vinaya (monastic vows). Much of the pedagogy involves extensive debating to refine understanding. The geshé curriculum has nearly a millennium of history dating back to the Kadampa master Geshé Langri Thangpa (Glang ri Thang pa), the author of *Eight Verses of Mind Training*, or *Blo sbyong tshigs brgyad ma*. In the last several years the Geshéma degree has been conferred to Gelugpa nuns.

2. The root Nāgārjuna text we used was from *Garland of Precious Explanations of the Meaning of Mūlamadhya-makakārikā* (*Dbu ma rtsa ba shes rab kyi ngag don bshad*

*pa rin po che'i phreng ba*) by Gyalwa Gendün Drup (Rgyal ba Dge 'dun grub), the First Dalai Lama.

3. Though it's often shortened to *Mūlamadhyamakakārikā*, the full Sanskrit title of *The Fundamental Verses on the Middle Way* is *Prajñānāmamūlamadhyamakakārikā*. The full Tibetan title is *Dbu ma rtsa ba tshig le'ur byas pa shes rab* or, for short, *Dbu ma rtsa ba'i shes rab*.

4. In the practice of highest yoga yantra, the final goal is the union of the two truths, the two bodies of a Buddha: the form body (Skt. *rūpakāya*) and the truth or wisdom body (Skt. *dharmakāya*). These are generated by cultivating the mind of clear light (Skt. *prabhāsvara*; Tib. *od gsal*) and the illusory body (Skt. *māyākāya*; Tib. *sgyu lus*). This union of the two bodies of a Buddha is the state of a vajradhāra. See also note 8.

5. Oral teaching in Bodh Gaya, 2018.

6. The tetralemma, called *catuṣkoti* in Sanskrit, is a form of reasoning commonly used in the classical logic of India. With respect to any logical proposition x, there are four and only four possibilities:

   1. affirmation,
   2. negation,
   3. both,
   4. neither.

   According to Garfield (2015a, 244–246), the insight behind the catuṣkoti is simply that truth values dispose themselves independently. While the only truth values are *true* and *false*—and all Buddhist philosophers of language insist on this fact—these truth values are independent of each other. A sentence may be (only) true; (only) false; *both* true and false; *neither* true nor false.

The catuṣkoti thus partitions logical space into four possibilities.

Within Indian logic, "Buddhist logic" has particularly focused on the fourfold negation, especially in the traditions of Nāgārjuna and the Madhyamaka school, but both positive and negative forms of the catuṣkoti are found.

Garfield says Nāgārjuna uses the catuṣkoti in two forms: positive and negative. In the positive form, usually from the conventional perspective, all four limbs are asserted. This means some sentences can be understood as true, false, both, and neither. For example, in chapter 18 verse 8 of *Fundamental Verses on the Middle Way,* he says the following:

> **Everything is real, and is not real.**
> **both real and not real,**
> **neither real nor not real.**
> **This is Lord Buddha's teaching.**

There are two readings of this verse. One reading is that each of these lines represents sequential stages in understanding. As Garfield says, one begins by urging people to take phenomena seriously. They are real. But then, in the second reading of this verse, it is important to teach that phenomena are in fact empty, that they do not exist as they appear to exist, and so they are unreal as they appear. Since this can lead to nihilism, it is important then to teach that their ultimate nonexistence is perfectly compatible with their conventional reality. Finally, it is necessary to urge that neither of these assertions conveys the ultimate reality of things, because that is beyond characterization by words. But this must be contrasted with the negative catuṣkoti, in which all four limbs are denied.

Nāgārjuna uses this negative catuṣkoti when discussing the ultimate perspective in chapter 22, verse 11:

> We do not assert "empty."
> We do not assert "non-empty."
> We assert neither both nor neither.
> These are used only nominally.

As Garfield shows, Nāgārjuna's point is that all language—no matter how useful—fails to characterize reality simply because it deals in unreal universals, superimposing concepts on a nonconceptualized world. To the extent that language is necessary at all, it is a necessary evil. While it can never succeed, it gives us the illusion that we have somehow encompassed the world as it is.

Richard Robinson (1957, 302–303) states that negativism is employed in amplification of the Greek tradition of philosophical skepticism, which consists of four members in a relation of exclusive disjunction—"one of, but not more than one of, 'a,' 'b,' 'c,' 'd,' is true." Buddhist dialecticians, from Gautama onward, have negated each of the alternatives and thus have negated the entire proposition. As these alternatives were supposedly exhaustive, their exhaustive negation has been termed "pure negation" and has been taken as evidence for the claim that Madhyamaka is negativism, or nihilism. Robinson fails to mention Nāgārjuna's positive use of the catuṣkoti.

7. *Ocean of Reasoning*, as translated in Samten and Garfield 2006, 93.

8. There is a difference here between the sūtra and tantra systems. The sūtra system, described above, tells us that when we investigate the nature of the self, the self disappears. The tantra system, on the other hand, maintains

that when we meditate on the emptiness of the deity, at the same time, the deity also appears to the mind. These occur simultaneously. This is the tantric practice of the indivisibility of the two truths, wisdom and method. In highest yoga tantra, the indivisible two truths is the union of the primordial clear light mind and the illusory body. At the resultant state, the union of the two truths is the union of the form and truth bodies of a buddha. They are recognized as indivisible, being of one nature. Paṇchen Sonam Drakpa (Paṇ chen Bsod nams grags pa) commented, based on his view of the *Guhyasamāja Tantra* (*Gsang 'dus rtsa rgyud*), that when one realizes the emptiness of the sprout, the appearance of the sprout disappears. However, when we meditate on the emptiness of the deity, the deity continues to appear. To explain this difference between sūtra and tantra, Paṇchen Sonam Drakpa draws the distinction between *pure* and *impure objects*. Impure objects are like a sprout, whereas pure objects are like the image of the deity. Pure objects, he argues, continue to appear even when recognized as empty.

9. With regard to the referent object, there are two different positions. Jamyang Shepa says our conceptions are not mistaken with respect to the referent object, but they are mistaken with respect to the appearing object. Most other Prāsaṅgika scholars take the position that our conceptions are mistaken with respect to the referent object. Therefore, most scholars maintain, analyzing the designated object, it must be the referent object to which we cling. It must be the object of our analysis. The goal of analyzing the designated object is to negate its true existence. We are not analyzing the ultimate "I" itself. Rather

we are analyzing the conventional object. But this *leads* to negating the ultimately existing "I." Thus, one approach is analyzing the conventional object in order to negate the ultimate object. The other analyzes the intrinsic existence of the object. Both ground their views in interpretations of the writings of Tsongkhapa.

10. Paṇchen Sönam Drakpa (Paṇ chen Bsod nams grags pa) lived in the fifteenth and sixteenth centuries and was the Fifteenth Ganden Tripa (Dga' ldan khri pa), or head of the Gelukpa tradition of Tibetan Buddhism. Paṇchen Sönam Drakpa was taught by the Second Dalai Lama, and in turn later became the teacher of the Third Dalai Lama. His collected works include fourteen volumes, constituting the main textbooks still used today in the educational curriculum of Drepung Loseling Monastic University, Ganden Shartse Monastic University, many monasteries in Kham and Amdo, and some monasteries in Mongolia.

11. Denma Tongpoen Rinpoché was one of the scholars who was instrumental in the translation of the *Mahāvibhāṣa* (for more on this key text, see note 16). His major disciples were Shakhor Khensur Nyima Rinpoché (Sha 'khor Mkhan zur nyi ma rin po che), Gen Pema Gyaltsen, and the late Denma Lochoe Rinpoché. His teacher was the previous Denma Lochoe Rinpoché.

12. Amdo Jigmé Damchö (A mdo 'Jigs med dam chos) lived from 1898 until 1946. He was a great contemporary Amdo lama who at age twenty-six wrote a book on the four noble truths in debate format called *The Roar of Fearless Reasoning* (*Bden pa bzhi las brtsams pa'i rtsod yig legs par bshad pa 'jigs med rigs pa'i gad rgyangs*). His collected works comprise about twenty volumes, including

a *lam rim* commentary on the *Path to Bliss*, and an annotated commentary on Tsongkhapa's insight section of *The Great Treatise on the Stages of the Path to Enlightenment.* He was a teacher to the Thirteenth Dalai Lama.

13. *Ocean of Reasoning*, as translated in Samten and Garfield 2006, 383.

14. *The Great Treatise on the Stages of the Path to Enlightenment*, as translated in Cutler and Newland 2002, vol. 3, 310, 6:166—6:167.

15. Ibid., 219, 6:13ab.

16. Gomang Geshé Akhu Sherap Gyatso (A khu Shes rab rgya mtsho) lived during the time of the Thirteenth Dalai Lama. He was a very learned translator who lived many years in China, where he eventually passed away. He began translating from Chinese into Tibetan the *Great Treasury of the Vaibhāṣikas* (*Mahāvibhāṣa*; *Bye brag bshad mdzod chen mo*), a very extensive and detailed explanation of the Vaibhāṣika tenet system. Atīśa Dīpaṃkara received teachings on this text for twelve years. Akhu Sherap Gyatso's translation was not completed before he died.

Shakhor Khensur Nyima Rinpoché and Gen Pema Gyaltsen's teacher, Geshé Denma Tongpoen from Drepung Loseling, were sent to China with a Chinese translator by the Thirteenth Dalai Lama for the specific purpose of translating this text in its entirety from Chinese into Tibetan. Yet the translation was still not completed. What was completed was offered to the Fourteenth Dalai Lama in the Potala Palace in Lhasa. When the Fourteenth Dalai Lama escaped abruptly in March 1959, the text was left behind and later partially destroyed.

More recently the Fourteenth Dalai Lama sent a Sera

Je Monastery geshé to Taiwan to complete the translation, possibly with the intention of adding it to the monastic curriculum. The translation is still in process at the time of this writing.

The Vaibhāṣikas claim this text to be a direct teaching from the Buddha. Others say an arhat composed this text, possibly around the time of the Buddha. The only significant text available today in Tibetan explaining the Vaibhāṣika tenet system is Vasubandhu's *Treasury of Abhidharma* (*Abhidharmakośa*), which mainly presents the Vaibhāṣika philosophical system.

Akhu Sherap Gyatso's main popularity comes from his *Pith Instructions* (*Man ngag*) lineage-holder status. This lineage comprises the generation and completion stages of the Guhyasamāja, Cakrasaṃvara, and Yamāntaka tantra systems of the highest yoga tantra.

17. For those readers who don't accept rebirth but who are interested in this analysis, the twelve links might provisionally be explained psychologically as a model of ordinary personal development, action, and perception. When grasping ends, so does desire.

18. Jones 2010, 58, I:35.

19. As translated in Cutler and Newland 2002, vol. 3, 296.

20. Garfield 2015a, 212–13.

21. The three bodies of a buddha are taught extensively in tantra, especially highest yoga tantra, but they are only superficially taught in the Sūtrayāna. There is the *dharmakāya*, which is the wisdom or truth body: the embodiment of the wisdom of the enlightened Buddha's mind. The dharmakāya is accessible only to other enlightened be-

ings. Then there is the *rūpakāya,* which is the form body, or the material embodiment of a buddha. The rūpakāya has two aspects, which together comprise the second and third of the bodies of a buddha.

The first aspect of the rūpakāya is the subtler *saṃbhogakāya,* or enjoyment body. Its nature is very subtle light energy with a corresponding subtle consciousness. It is accessible only to highly realized beings such as ārya bodhisattvas, who have directly realized emptiness and are on the bodhisattva Vajrayāna path. Out of his immense compassion, the Buddha also manifests in a more gross form: the second aspect of the rūpakāya, which is accessible to ordinary beings like us, so that we can see him and hear his teachings. It is called the *nirmāṇakāya,* or emanation body. Śākyamuni Buddha was a nirmāṇakāya emanation.

The three bodies of a Buddha can be explained in demystified language; they can be seen as metaphors for three embodiments of awakening. One can embody awakening in physical actions, in wisdom or understanding, and in one's happiness and release from suffering.

22. The *eight kinds of persons* refer to the attainers and enterers of the path mentioned in the preceding verse. The four fruits are the fruits of a stream-enterer, a once-returner, a nonreturner, and an arhat. The four who enter the path are those on the paths toward attaining the four fruits. (See also the Dalai Lama 2009, note 33.)

23. Garfield 2015a, 261.

24. Ibid., 112.

25. *The Great Treatise on the Stages to the Path of Enlightenment,*

as translated in Cutler and Newland 2002, vol. 3, 280–281, 6:152–57.

26. Ibid., 282, 6:156.

27. Ibid., 286.

28. Ibid., 287.

29. Jinpa 2006, 9.

30. *Ocean of Reasoning*, as translated in Samten and Garfield 2006, 449. The twelve views are that the world is eternal, is not eternal, is both, is neither; that the world is finite, is infinite, is both, is neither; that the Tathāgata, after parinirvāṇa, exists, does not exist, both exists and not exists, and neither exists nor not exists.

31. Jinpa n.d., *In Praise of Dependent Origination*, 1 and 4.

32. Here I am using the Tibetan translation and will continue to do so when commenting on the root text, for I made great use of *Garland of Precious Explanations of the Meaning of Mūlamadhyamakakārikā* by the First Dalai Lama.

33. The first Künkhyen Jamyang Shepa (Kun mkhyen 'Jam dbyang bzhad pa) Ngawang Tsondru was born in 1648 and died in 1721. His *Presentation of Tenets: Lion's Roar Eradicating Error, Precious Lamp Illuminating the Genuine Path to Omniscience*, commonly known among scholars as *Drupta Chenmo (The Great Exposition of Tenets)*, and other texts such as *The Port of Entry of the Fortunate: A Decisive Argument on the Madhyamakāvatāra, the Treasury of Scripture and Reason Revealing the Profound Meaning (Dbu ma la 'jug pa'i mtha' dpyod lung rigs gter mdzod zab don kun gsal skal bzang 'jug ngogs)*, commonly known as *Uma Chenpo (Dbu ma chen po)*, *The Great Exposition of Madhyamakāvatāra (Entering the Middle Way)* are the primary text books for Drepung Gomang, Labrang, and

some Mongolian monasteries. He lived during the time of the 5th Dalai Lama.

34. *Ocean of Reasoning*, as translated in Samten and Garfield 2006, 62, 161b.

35. *Ocean of Reasoning*, as translated in Samten and Garfield 2006, 62–63.

36. Samten and Garfield offer clear explanations in their translation of Tsongkhapa's *Ocean of Reasoning* (2006, 61–66). However, they suggest we refer to the extensive explanations found in Tsongkhapa's *The Essence of Eloquent Interpretation*. Tsongkhapa offers additional detailed explanations in *The Great Treatise on the Stages to the Path of Enlightenment* (Cutler and Newland 2002, vol. 3, 225–75).

37. *Ocean of Reasoning*, as translated in Samten and Garfield 2006, 93, 14:13.

38. Ibid., 95, 285b.

39. In the Sanskrit version, "just as a track is not seen in the sky."

40. Ibid.

41. Ibid., 96, 261b.

42. Thurman 1991.

43. Chone Rinpoché's text is sometimes referred to as *The Small Essence of Eloquent Interpretation* (*Lekshe nyingpo chungwa*). It has not been translated into English.

44. Tsongkapa 2006, 97.

45. Ibid., 98.

46. Ibid.

47. Ibid., 99.

48. Ibid., 96.

# BIBLIOGRAPHY

Batchelor, Stephen, trans. 1979. *A Guide to the Bodhisattva's Way of Life*. Dharamsala: Library of Tibetan Works and Archives.

Bitbol, M. 2003. "A Cure for Metaphysical Illusions: Kant, Quantum Mechanics, and the Madhyamaka." In *Buddhism and Science*, edited by B. Alan Wallace. New York: Columbia University Press.

Brefcynski-Lewis, J. A., A. Lutz, H. S. Schaefer, D. B. Levinson, and R. J. Davidson. 2007. "Neural Correlates of Attentional Expertise in Long-Term Meditation Practitioners." *Proceedings of the National Academy of Sciences* 104 (27): 11483–11488.

Cabezón, José Ignacio. 1992. *A Dose of Emptiness: An Annotated Translation of the sTong thun chen mo of mKhas grub dGe legs dpal bzang*. Albany: State University of New York Press.

Chandrakīrti. 2005. *Introduction to the Middle Way: Chandrakirti's Madhyamakavatara*. With commentary by Jamgön

Mipham. Translated by the Padmakara Translation Group. Boston: Shambhala Publications.

Conze, Edward, trans. 1973. *The Perfection of Wisdom in Eight Thousand Lines and Its Verse Summary*. San Francisco: Four Seasons Foundation.

Cowherds. 2011. *Moonshadows: Conventional Truth in Buddhist Philosophy*. New York: Oxford University Press.

Crosby, Kate, and Andrew Skilton, trans. 1995. *Śāntideva: The Bodhicaryāvatāra*. New York: Oxford University Press.

Cutler, Joshua W. C., and Guy Newland, eds. 2000–2004. *The Great Treatise on the Stages of the Path to Enlightenment*. By Tsongkhapa. 3 vols. Translated by the Lamrim Chenmo Translation Committee. Ithaca, NY: Snow Lion Publications.

Dalai Lama (Tenzin Gyatso). 1997. *The Four Noble Truths*. Translated by Thupten Jinpa. London: Thorsons.

———. 2000. *Dzogchen: Heart Essence of the Great Perfection*. Translated by Geshé Thupten Jinpa and Richard Barron. Edited by Patrick Gaffney. Ithaca: Snow Lion Publications.

———. 2001. *Ethics for the New Millennium*. New York: Riverhead Books.

———. 2002. *Essence of the Heart Sūtra: The Dalai Lama's Heart of Wisdom Teachings*. Translated and edited by Geshé Thupten Jinpa. Boston: Wisdom Publications.

———. 2005. *Practicing Wisdom: The Perfection of Shantideva's Bodhisattva Way*. Translated and edited by Geshé Thupten Jinpa. Boston: Wisdom Publications.

———. 2009. *The Middle Way: Faith Grounded in Reason*. Translated by Thupten Jinpa. Somerville, MA: Wisdom Publications.

Dreyfus, Georges B. J. 1997. *Recognizing Reality: Dharmakīrti's Philosophy and Its Tibetan Interpretations.* Albany, NY: State University of New York Press.

———. 2003. *The Sound of Two Hands Clapping: The Education of a Tibetan Buddhist Monk.* Berkeley: University of California Press.

Dreyfus, Georges B. J., and Sara L. McClintock, eds. 2003. *The Svātrantika-Prāsaṅgika Distinction: What Difference Does a Difference Make?* Boston: Wisdom Publications.

Dunne, John D. 2004. *Foundations of Dharmakīrti's Philosophy.* Boston: Wisdom Publications.

Dunne, John, and Sara McClintock, trans. 1997. *The Precious Garland: An Epistle to a King.* Boston: Wisdom Publications.

Gallagher, Shaun. 2007. "Neurophilosophy and Neurophenomenology." *Phenomenology 2005* 5 (1): 293–316. Bucharest: Zeta Press.

———, ed. 2011. *The Oxford Handbook of the Self.* New York: Oxford University Press.

Gallagher, Shaun, and Dan Zahavi. 2012. *The Phenomenological Mind.* 2nd ed. New York: Routledge.

Garfield, Jay L. 1994. "Dependent Co-origination and the Emptiness of Emptiness: Why Did Nāgārjuna Begin with Causation?" *Philosophy East and West* 44: 219–250.

———, trans. 1995. *The Fundamental Wisdom of the Middle Way: Nāgārjuna's Mūlamadhyamakakārikā.* New York: Oxford University Press.

———. 2001. "Nāgārjuna's Theory of Causality: Implications Sacred and Profane." *Philosophy East and West* 51 (4): 507–524.

———. 2002. *Empty Words: Buddhist Philosophy and Cross-Cultural Interpretation*. New York: Oxford University Press.

———. 2014. "Madhyamaka, Nihilism, and the Emptiness of Emptiness." In *Nothingness in Asian Philosophy*, edited by JeeLoo Liu and Douglas L. Berger, 44–54. London: Routledge.

———. 2015a. *Engaging Buddhism: Why It Matters to Philosophy*. New York: Oxford University Press.

———. 2015b. "Buddhist Ethics in the Context of Conventional Truth: Path and Transformation." In *Moonpaths: Ethics and Emptiness*, edited by the Cowherds, 77–96. New York: Oxford University Press.

Garfield, Jay L., and William Edelglass, eds. 2011. *The Oxford Handbook of World Philosophy*. New York: Oxford University Press.

Garfield, Jay L., and Graham Priest. 2003. "Nāgārjuna and the Limits of Thought." *Philosophy East and West* 53 (1): 1–21.

Gen 'dun grub. 1987. *Garland of Precious Explanations of the Meaning of Mūlamadhyamakakārikā, Dbu ma rtsa ba shes rab kyi don bshad pa rin po che'i phreng ba*. Sarnath: Gelugpa Student Welfare Committee.

Guenther, Herbert V. 1976. *Buddhist Philosophy in Theory and Practice*. Boston: Shambhala Publications.

Gyatso, Lobsang, and Graham Woodhouse. 2011. *Tsongkhapa's Praise for Dependent Relativity*. Boston: Wisdom Publications.

Hopkins, Jeffrey. 1996. *Meditation on Emptiness*. Somerville, MA: Wisdom Publications.

Huntington, C. W., Jr. 1989. *The Emptiness of Emptiness: An Introduction to Early Indian Mādhyamika*. With Geshé

Namgyal Wangchen. Honolulu: University of Hawaii Press.

Inada, Kenneth K., trans. 1970. *Nāgārjuna: A Translation of His Mūlamadhyamakakārikā with an Introductory Essay.* Buffalo: State University of New York Press.

Jinpa, Thupten. 2002. *Self, Reality and Reason in Tibetan Philosophy: Tsongkhapa's Quest for the Middle Way.* London: Routledge Curzon.

———, trans. 2003. *Three Principal Aspects of the Path.* Unpublished.

———, trans. 2006. *A Commentary on the Awakening Mind.* By Nāgārjuna. http://www.tibetanclassics.org/html-assets /Awakening%20Mind%20Commentary.pdf

———, trans. 2014. *In Praise of Dependent Origination.* By Je Tsongkhapa. http://www.tibetanclassics.org/html-assets /In%20Praise%20of%20Dependent%20Origination.pdf.

———, trans. n.d. *In Praise of Dependent Origination.* By Je Tsongkhapa. http://www.tibetanclassics.org/html-assets/ In%20Praise%20of%20Dependent%20Origination.pdf

———, trans. n.d. *Sixty Stanzas of Reasoning.* By Nāgārjuna. http://www.tibetanclassics.org/html-assets/SixtyStanzas .pdf

Jones, Richard H., trans. 2010. *Nāgārjuna: Buddhism's Most Important Philosopher.* New York: Jackson Square Books.

Kalupahana, David J. 1976. *Buddhist Philosophy: A Historical Analysis.* Honolulu: University of Hawaii Press.

Kant, Immanuel. 1965. *Critique of Pure Reason.* Translated by N.K. Smith. New York: St. Martin's Press.

Kasulis, T. P. 1983. *Zen Action/Zen Person.* Honolulu: University of Hawaii Press.

Katsura, Shōryū, ed. 1999. *Dharmakīrti's Thought and Its*

*Impact on Indian and Tibetan Philosophy: Proceedings of the Third International Dharmakīrti Conference, Hiroshima, November 4–6, 1997.* Vienna: Verlag der Österreichisschen Akademie der Wissenschaften.

Keown, Damien. 2005. *Buddhist Ethics: A Very Short Introduction.* New York: Oxford University Press.

Komito, David Ross, and Ven. Tenzin Dorjee, trans. 1987. *Nāgārjuna's Seventy Stanzas: A Buddhist Psychology of Emptiness.* With commentary by Geshé Sonam Rinchen. Ithaca, NY: Snow Lion Publications.

Lang, Karen C., trans. 2003. *Four Illusions: Candrakīrti's Advice for Those on the Bodhisattva Path.* New York: Oxford University Press.

Loizzo, Joseph, trans. 2007. *Nāgārjuna's Reason Sixty "Yuktiṣaṣṭikā" with Candrakīrti's Commentary "Yuktiṣaṣṭikāvṛtti."* New York: Columbia University Press.

Lutz, Antoine, John D. Dunne, and Richard J. Davidson. 2007. "Meditation and the Neuroscience of Consciousness: An Introduction." In *The Cambridge Handbook of Consciousness,* edited by Philip David Zelazo, Morris Moscovitch, and Evan Thompson, 499–554. New York: Cambridge University Press.

Lutz, Antoine, and Evan Thompson. 2003. "Neurophenomenology: Integrating Subjective Experience and Brain Dynamics in the Neuroscience of Consciousness." *Journal of Consciousness Studies* 10 (9–10): 31–52.

Merleau-Ponty, M. 1962. *The Phenomenology of Perception.* Translated by Colin Smith. London: Routledge & Kegan Paul.

Patsab Nyima Drak, Mahāsumati, and Kanakavarman, trans.

2003. *Prasannapadā.* Sarnath: Gelugpa Students' Welfare Committee. 32: xvii.

Powers, John. 2007. *Introduction to Tibetan Buddhism.* 2nd ed. Ithaca, NY: Snow Lion Publications.

Robinson, Richard. 1957. "Some Logical Aspects of Nāgārjuna's System." *Philosophy East and West* 6 (4): 291–308.

Samten, Geshé Ngawang, and Jay L. Garfield, trans. 2006. *Ocean of Reasoning: A Great Commentary on Nāgārjuna's Mūlamadhyamakakārikā.* By Rje Tsong Khapa. Oxford: Oxford University Press.

Shantideva (1979). *Guide to the Bodhisattva's Way of Life (Bodhisattvacharyavatara).* Stephen Batchelor (trans.). Dharamsala: Library of Tibetan Works and Archives.

Shantideva (1995). *The Bodhicāryavatara.* Kate Crosby and Andrew Skilton (trans.). New York: Oxford University Press.

Shantideva (1997). *A Guide to the Bodhisattva's Way of Life (Bodhisattvacharyavatara).* V.A. Wallace and B.A. Wallace (trans. from Sanskrit and Tibetan). Ithaca: Snow Lion Publications.

Siderits, Mark, and Shōryū Katsura, trans. 2013. *Nāgārjuna's Middle Way: Mūlamadhyamakakārikā.* Boston: Wisdom Publications.

Siderits, Mark, Evan Thompson, and Dan Zahavi, eds. 2013. *Self? No Self?: Perspectives from Analytical, Phenomenological, and Indian Traditions.* New York: Oxford University Press.

Sprung, Mervyn, trans. 1979. *Lucid Exposition of the Middle Way: The Essential Chapters from the Prasannapadā of Chandrakīrti Translated from the Sanskrit.* In collaboration with T. R. V. Murti and U. S. Vyas. London: Routledge & Kegan Paul.

Tanahashi, Kazuaki, ed. 1985. "Actualizing the Fundamental Point: *Genjō Kōan*" In *Moon in a Dewdrop: Writings of Zen Master Dōgen.* Translated by Robert Aiken et al., 69–73. New York: North Point Press.

Thompson, Evan. 2006. "Neurophenomenology and Contemplative Experience." In *The Oxford Handbook of Religion and Science*, edited by Philip Clayton with the assistance of Zachary Simpson. New York: Oxford University Press.

———. 2007. *Mind in Life: Biology, Phenomenology, and the Sciences of Mind.* Cambridge, MA: The Belknap Press of Harvard University Press.

Thompson, Evan, Antoine Lutz, and Diego Cosmelli. 2005. "Neurophenomenology: An Introduction for Neurophilosophers." In *Cognition and the Brain: The Philosophy and Neuroscience Movement*, edited by Andrew Brook and Kathleen Akins, 40–97. Cambridge: Cambridge University Press.

Thompson, Evan, and Dan Zahavi. 2007. "Philosophical Issues: Phenomenology." In *The Cambridge Handbook of Consciousness*, edited by Philip David Zalazo, Morris Moscovitch, and Evan Thompson, 67–88. New York: Cambridge University Press.

Thurman, Robert A. F., trans. 1976. *The Holy Teaching of Vimalakīrti: A Mahāyāna Scripture.* University Park: Pennsylvania State University Press.

———. 1984. *The Central Philosophy of Tibet: A Study and Translation of Jey Tsong Khapa's "Essence of True Eloquence."* Princeton: Princeton University Press.

————. 2005. *The Jewel Tree of Tibet: The Enlightenment Engine of Tibetan Buddhism*. New York: Simon & Schuster.

————. 2006. *Life and Teachings of Tsong Khapa*. Dharamsala: Library for Tibetan Works and Archives.

————. 2011. "The Politics of Enlightenment." In *Becoming Buddha: Wisdom Culture for a Meaningful Life*, edited by Renuka Singh, 149–182. New Delhi: Penguin Ananda.

Tillmann, J. S., and Acharya T. Tsering, trans. 1997. *Commentary on the "Entry into the Middle" Lamp which Elucidates Reality*. Varanasi: Central Institute of Higher Tibetan Studies.

Tsering, T., and J. S. Tillmann, trans. 2012. *Autocommentary on the "Introduction to the Centre."* Varanasi: Sattanam.

Varela, Francisco J. 1999. "The Specious Present: A Neurophenomenology of Time Consciousness." In *Naturalizing Phenomenology: Issues in Contemporary Phenomenology and Cognitive Science*, edited by Jean Petitot, Francisco J. Varela, Bernard Pachoud, and Jean-Michel Roy, 266–314. Stanford: Stanford University Press.

Varela, F. J., and E. Thompson. 2003. "Neural Synchrony and the Unity of Mind: A Neurophenomenological Perspective." In *The Unity of Consciousness: Binding, Integration, and Dissociation*, edited by Axel Cleeremans, 266–287. New York: Oxford University Press.

Wallace, B. Alan, ed. 2003. *Buddhism and Science: Breaking New Ground*. New York: Columbia University Press.

————. 2009. *Contemplative Science: Where Buddhism and Neuroscience Converge*. New York: Columbia University Press.

Wallace, B. Alan, and Brian Hodel. 2008. *Embracing Mind:*

*The Common Ground of Science and Spirituality*. Boston: Shambhala Publications.

Wallace, Vesna A., and B. Alan Wallace, trans. 1997. *A Guide to the Bodhisattva's Way of Life (Bodhisattvacharyavatara)*. By Śāntideva. Ithaca, NY: Snow Lion Publications.

Walser, Joseph. 2005. *Nāgārjuna in Context: Mahāyāna Buddhism and Early Indian Culture*. New York: Columbia University Press.

Williams, Paul. 2009. *Mahāyāna Buddhism: The Doctrinal Foundations*. 2nd ed. New York: Routledge.

Zelazo, Philip David, Morris Moscovitch, and Evan Thompson, eds. 2007. *The Cambridge Handbook of Consciousness*. New York: Cambridge University Press.

# INDEX

## A

Abhidharma, 22, 169n1

*Abhidharmakośa. See* Vasubandhu, *Treasury of Abhidharma* (*Abhidharmakośa*)

absurd consequences, 86–87, 122, 118–19, 121–22, 123, 124, 128, 129, 138

action, 45, 176n17
four noble truths and, 71
moral and immoral, distinguishing, 63, 85–86
of producing an effect, 111, 118, 135–37
reification and, 65, 85–86
as root of cyclic existence, 43
three types, 39
*See also* karma

affirming negative, 127

afflictions, 12, 69, 99

aggregates, five

and Buddha, analysis of, 90, 91, 94–95, 101–3
cooperative cause of, 42–43
existence and, 40
self and, 14, 47–48, 50–51, 53–54, 115
suffering of, 44
variant views of, 50–51

aging, 38, 40, 44, 116

Akhu Sherap Gyatso, Gomang Geshé, 34, 175n16

Amdo Jigmé Damchö, 20, 174n12

analogies and examples
blue color, 28–29, 133–34, 143
car, 13
catching poisonous snake, 64, 77
clay pot, 130
cloth from thread, 145, 146, 147, 149
darkness from flame, 121

# ABOUT THE AUTHOR

Barry Kerzin is an affiliate professor at the University of Washington Tacoma, a visiting professor at Central University of Tibetan Studies in Varanasi, India, an honorary professor at the University of Hong Kong, and a former assistant professor of medicine at the University of Washington. Barry is also a fellow at the Mind and Life Institute and consults for the Max Planck Institute in Leipzig on compassion training. He is the founder and president of the Altruism in Medicine Institute and the founder and chairman of the Human Values Institute in Japan. He was ordained as a monk by the Dalai Lama, and for thirty years he has been providing free medical care to everyone from the poor up to the highest lamas—including the Dalai Lama. After completing many meditation retreats, his brain was studied to assess structural and functional changes.

He has written *No Fear No Death: The Transformative Power of Compassion* and, in Japanese, *Tibetan Buddhist Prescription for Happiness,* and with the Dalai Lama and Professor Tonagawa, *Mind and Matter: Dialogue between Two Nobel Laureates* in Japanese.

**The Middle Way**
*Faith Grounded in Reason*
His Holiness the Dalai Lama
Translated by Thupten Jinpa

"How fortunate we are to have access to these brilliant teachings given by the Dalai Lama. A truly inspiring book."—*Mandala*

**Nāgārjuna's Middle Way**
*Mūlamadhyamakakārikā*
Mark Siderits and Shōryū Katsura

"Authoritative, vivid, and illuminating."—Graham Priest, author of *Logic: A Very Short Introduction*

**The Buddhist Philosophy of the Middle**
*Essays on Indian and Tibetan Madhyamaka*
David Seyfort Ruegg
Foreword by Tom Tillemans

"Without a doubt, the articles collected here will greatly advance this philosophical tradition finding its rightful place as one of the treasures of human thought and reflection."—Ernst Steinkellner, University of Vienna

**Emptiness**
*The Foundation of Buddhist Thought, Volume 5*
Geshe Tashi Tsering with Gordon McDougall
Foreword by Lama Zopa Rinpoche

"Geshe Tashi's systematic approach to Buddhist thought allows readers to gradually but surely enhance their knowledge of Buddhism without feeling overwhelmed."
—*Eastern Horizon*

# About Wisdom Publications

Wisdom Publications is the leading publisher of classic and contemporary Buddhist books and practical works on mindfulness. To learn more about us or to explore our other books, please visit our website at wisdompubs.org or contact us at the address below.

Wisdom Publications
199 Elm Street
Somerville, MA 02144 USA

We are a 501(c)(3) organization, and donations in support of our mission are tax deductible.

Wisdom Publications is affiliated with the Foundation for the Preservation of the Mahayana Tradition (FPMT).